Build it

Build it

The Rebel Playbook for World-Class Employee Engagement

Glenn Elliott and Debra Corey

WILEY

This edition first published 2018

© 2018 Glenn Elliott and Debra Corey.

Registered office

John Wiley & Sons Ltd, The Atrium, Southern Gate, Chichester, West Sussex, PO19 8SQ, United Kingdom

For details of our global editorial offices, for customer services and for information about how to apply for permission to reuse the copyright material in this book please see our website at www.wiley.com.

Library of Congress Cataloging-in-Publication Data is Available:

ISBN 9781119390053 (Hardcover)
ISBN 9781119390084 (ePDF)
ISBN 9781119390077 (ePub)

Cover design: Sevi Rahimova & Leonie Williamson

Set in 12/15pt and JansonTextLTStd by SPi Global, Chennai, India

Printed in Great Britain by TJ International Ltd, Padstow, Cornwall, UK

10 9 8 7 6 5 4 3 2

To the rebels, the misfits, the troublemakers.
Let's make the world a better place to work.

Contents

Alphabetical List of Plays

1

Understanding Employee Engagement

Chapter Objectives

In this chapter, we will:

- Establish the proven link between employee engagement and competitive advantage.
- Define employee engagement and understand how engaged employees add value.
- Discuss the changes that technology is bringing to our economy that make action urgent and critical.

Key Points

- This is a practical book based on real company experiences for anyone who wants to improve their business, regardless of their role or job level.
- You will have to rebel against *standard practice*—the status quo has failed and rebelling is the only way to make a difference.
- Don't confuse employee engagement with employee happiness; they are fundamentally different.
- Don't get hung up on jargon—engagement, experience, organizational health; it's not important. Just get started on the journey.

Introduction

A group of companies has twice the stock market performance of their peers. They innovate more, deliver better customer service and have half the employee turnover. They rebel against the status quo by treating people differently, and they've been rewarded with productivity and bottom-line results that leave other companies behind. They are the companies with the most engaged workforces—measured and tracked by numerous surveys and indexes, with the data proving the connection to real business results.

These companies have found a way to build an engaging culture—a culture where hard-working people thrive in jobs with challenge and excitement. A culture where people regularly put their companies and their customers ahead of their own needs. These companies have been outperforming their peers for nearly 20 years.

Of all the things we do in modern business, the link between employee engagement and business results is one of the most clearly proven. Gallup, Great Place to Work, Best Companies and Glassdoor all analyze employee engagement and correlate it to stock market performance. Whichever data you look at, the results are the same— companies with engaged employees beat their competition.

The Gallup index alone has 30 million data points going back nearly two decades: They interview 500 American adults every day, collecting data on employee engagement 350 days of the year.[1] The truth is, we proved the link between employee engagement and business performance years ago. **Now it's time to act!**

---

[1]http://www.gallup.com/201194/gallup-daily-work.aspx

Big Companies Can Correlate Performance Directly to Engagement

With 85,000 staff across nearly 1,000 stores, UK retailer Marks & Spencer has plenty of data to crunch.[2]

Stores in the top quartile for employee engagement are twice as likely to achieve the highest service rating and have 25% less staff absence compared to stores in the bottom quartile.

It turns out that engaged employees deliver better customer service and take less time off sick. Surprised? You shouldn't be.

Yet, despite this robust evidence, the vast majority of companies are either doing nothing, or not enough, to engage their staff. The lack of progress causes consultants to invent new ways of saying the same thing: *"Engagement is dead, long live employee experience," "Forget engagement think about organizational health"*—but actually it's all broadly the same thing.

The problem with employee engagement isn't what we're calling it. The problem is we're failing to make the necessary fundamental changes to our disengaging workplace practices.

The majority of our organizations are nothing without the collective output, ingenuity, choices and decisions of our staff. Company culture is simply the term that describes how you treat people and how you set the conditions in which they do

---

[2]https://www.etsplc.com/ms-employee-survey-case-study/

their work. To fix company culture and allow people to choose engagement, we don't need fancy initiatives around the edges; we need to fundamentally change how we treat the people who work for us.

When the *Harvard Business Review* surveyed business leaders in 2014, 71% of them said employee engagement was *critical* to the success of their organizations, but only 24% of these same leaders said their workforces were highly engaged. This difference is what we call the *engagement gap*.

No matter how you gather, track or slice the data, the big picture is that almost three-quarters of our employees simply don't care much about our companies, they don't care much about our customers, and they're not really working as well or as hard as they could be. We've written this book to help you change that. We've written this book to help you make the world a better place to work.

The Business Case for Employee Engagement Has Been Made

Engagement is proven to deliver business results. Many leaders seem to know that, but companies still struggle to take meaningful and effective actions to make things better.

Understanding Employee Engagement

Just about every vendor in HR describes themselves as an employee engagement platform or product these days—even the payroll companies! You could easily be forgiven for thinking this is a new trend that's just started; an invention of new technology.

But the truth is that we've known for over 100 years that **treating people better gets better business results**. It's important to focus on those words, so let's repeat them: "**Treating people better gets better business results**." We have disengaged employees because we lie to them; treat them as adversaries; and give them crappy jobs without autonomy, excitement or accountability. The Engagement Bridge™ model will help you understand the things that cause disengagement, and show you the tools and strategies to address them.

If you're reading this thinking that you've already done work on engagement and it didn't work, ask yourself: Did you really change how your organization treats people? Because if you only focused around the edges—installing a new intranet, a tool that helps staff know whose birthday it is, or something to count how many steps they walked—then nice as that is, it won't have been enough.

For our purposes, we've always believed in a results-focused definition of engagement. We define someone as engaged when they:

1. **Understand and believe in the direction the organization is going**—its purpose, mission and objectives—so they feel part of something bigger than themselves.
2. **Understand how their role affects and contributes** to the organization's purpose, mission and objectives.
3. **Genuinely want the organization to succeed** and feel shared success with the organization. They will often put the organization's needs ahead of their own.

You'll find that engaged employees build *better, stronger and more resilient organizations*. They do this in three ways:

1. **Engaged employees make better decisions** because they understand more about the organization, their customers and the context they are operating in.

2. **Engaged employees are more productive** because they like or love what they are doing—they waste less time and get less distracted by things that don't further the organization's mission or goals.

3. **Engaged employees innovate more** because they deeply want the organization to succeed.

It's easy to get *happiness* and *engagement* confused, and it's also common to think that a good employer creates an *easy* place to work. Neither is true.

You do not need employee engagement to have happy employees. I've found companies that have quite happy employees based on a combination of good working conditions, low ambition and low accountability for results. This tends to result in the best people leaving and an average group of people staying and finding meaning and self-actualization outside of work. It's pretty dreadful for organizational performance, and you can guarantee those companies won't have the durable and resilient cultures needed to navigate the tough years ahead.

Engagement is something deeper, more meaningful for the employee and more valuable to the organization. With the pace of business accelerating by the day, we need engaged employees more than ever.

The Case for Action

Technology is making the world move faster, and when the world goes faster, competition gets harder. Companies are innovating and changing at a rate previously unimagined. Product lifecycles are shorter, links between manufacturing and the customer are closer, and the demands for process improvement and process change have never been greater. We've never needed our staff on our side more than we do now.

Just look at the time taken for new products to reach 50 million users. Radio was invented at the start of the 20th century and it took 38 years to reach 50 million listeners, but 100 years later, it took just four years for the iPod to reach the same size audience. It took just three years for the internet, a year for Facebook and a month for *Angry Birds*!

Time to reach **50 million** users

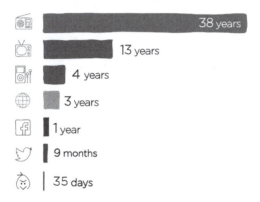

This speed generally makes better outcomes for the customer, but it also brings huge instability. With technology, new players with small, highly engaged teams can outmaneuver and outperform their larger, slower competitors—look what happened to Nokia, Polaroid, Blockbuster and Borders. Each of these companies failed because when the winds changed, they couldn't move fast enough, reorganize themselves quickly enough or stay connected to the customer closely enough. You could say they all failed because of a failure of their corporate cultures.

Great cultures are full of openness, honesty, courage, connection to the customer, and vast swathes of passionate, engaged employees—these are the cultures that enable companies to react and respond to fast-changing markets and fast-changing environments.

> ## How Can We Get Customers to Love Us If Our Employees Don't Even Like Us?
>
> In the new, supercharged, super-fast, super-competitive economy, we need customers to love our brands, love our products and advocate for our companies.
>
> Surely customer love must start with employee love?

Ultimately, Engagement is a Choice

Employee engagement isn't something just for rich tech companies, and it isn't something just for companies that employ lots of young people, either. Everyone, regardless of age, deserves to have a job they love that makes them feel fulfilled, and every company needs its people on side more than ever.

When I worked for a major public company in the 1990s, despite the fact we were all shareholders (so you'd think we'd automatically be engaged), I never felt more distant from the ability or desire to make an impact.

But when I met Lei, who works at the El Cortez Hotel and Casino in downtown Las Vegas, I heard a very different story. He had been running the roulette table for 25 years and told me that El Cortez was a good employer, a good company that treated him well. He was engaged, so he knew how to make the company successful.

> *"If I treat the customers well and smile and wish them luck, then they come back. I want that. There's a lot of other casinos on Fremont Street where customers can spend their money, and I want them to come here. This is a good job. I want to keep it, I want the casino to still be here."*

I've also seen that employee engagement can be developed in the harshest of conditions. In 2013, GM Holden, an Australian car company, announced that the entire manufacturing plant would close, marking the end of domestic car production in the country. But the exceptional efforts on engagement made by local leaders ensured that every key production and engagement metric improved, with every employee dedicated to ensuring that the last car that rolled off the production line would be their very best ever.

This shows that there is no industry you must be in, no sector you must be from, and no age or stage your company must be at—you can make employee engagement work for you and make a real difference.

Employee Engagement is a Journey, Not a Destination

Don't worry for a second about where you are—only care that you are actually moving, making small changes and moving in the right direction.

Employee engagement is never done or perfect, but you'll be surprised at the results you get with even a little bit of effort.

And remember, the bar for success is remarkably low—most companies are pretty average, as the engagement stats show. If you can get even 20% better at two or three elements in the Engagement Bridge™, you'll really be able to see competitive advantage through your people.

Getting Started

Don't read too much into the order of chapters in this book. The truth is you need to understand the elements in the Bridge™ and then decide what is urgent and pressing for you.

To make things easier and provide inspiration, half of the book is dedicated to the case studies, or *plays*—this is a *playbook*, after all. Debra led on the plays and interviewed hundreds of companies in her research over the last two years. As well as the plays in this book, you can find dozens more on the book's website, rebelplaybook.com.

We've chosen plays from companies big and small, young and mature, with big budgets and with small budgets, and often no budgets. We found you don't have to be a VC-fueled startup or a well-funded corporation to get amazing results from your people. We've also chosen plays from all types of rebels—some taking small steps and others taking bigger steps into their *"rebelution"*—to make the point that there are lots of different ways to be a rebel.

Some of the things in this book may sound outlandish and you might think you could never do them at your company. It's important to remember that this is a *Rebel Playbook*. The status quo of how we treat people at work has failed and we *need* to get out of our comfort zones to make an impact. If some parts make you feel a little uncomfortable, that's OK—use it to power your own *rebelution* at work.

Don't despair if the overall task looks big and, for heaven's sake, don't give up. Employee engagement isn't binary: You're never done or not done. Instead, think of it as moving forward or moving backward. It's a journey that you never complete, but the most important thing to do is to get moving.

2

Introducing the
Engagement Bridge™

Chapter Objectives

In this chapter, we will:

- Unpack the Engagement Bridge™ and look at each of the 10 elements.
- Show how the elements relate to each other and explain the difference between the connecting elements and the underpinning elements.
- Discuss where to start on your employee engagement journey.

Key Points

- The Engagement Bridge™ is a 10-part model to help you identify and improve the levers of employee engagement in your company.
- The model gives you the areas to look at, ideas and tools. Ultimately you should focus your work where you can make an impact.
- Start where you can act fastest—don't squander time. What's important is direction of travel and velocity, not order. The model requires a "bias for action."
- Engagement is not binary and you never reach perfection. But that's OK—the more effort you put in, the more you get out.

Introduction

The Engagement Bridge™ is a model to help you think about the ways your organization influences the people who work for you. The goal is to help you create the conditions that will allow your people to engage with their jobs and your organization. We spent 10 years developing the model through our work with more than 2,000 companies worldwide, and you can use it to develop an employee engagement plan that works for you.

There are 10 Elements in the Engagement Bridge™

Seven of them connect your organization with your people and three are special—they underpin and support the bridge. These underpinnings elements are Pay & Benefits, Workspace, and Wellbeing—without them, your bridge is on shaky ground.

The distinction is key—the underpinning elements don't cross the divide—and you cannot engage your workforce with these elements alone. They are critically important and the absence of them can destroy completely any chances of engagement. If we're looking for what to blame for the lack of engagement improvement in the last 10 years, then top of my list would be the myth that a fancy office and some perks are all you need. They are useful, but only a step in your journey.

Imagine a bridge crossing over a running stream. You need to get your people over the water, and the elements on the bridge are like beams of wood to help you do this. You can bridge the stream with any one beam, but with only one, you can't get many people across at once and it's wobbly and unsafe. Add a second and things get better; add a third or a fourth and you're really getting somewhere.

But the banks of your stream are muddy and slippery, and you need a decent base or your beams can slide in and be washed away. That's where the underpinning elements come in—by acting as rocks. These rocks give you a stable base to build on. Without them, it's hard to even get started.

If you try to build a bridge with rocks alone, you'll fail. And if you build a bridge with too few beams of wood, it won't last, either. All of the pieces are valuable, and together they create a strong and enduring structure. How important or urgent each element is depends on your organization, your context, your situation.

Connecting Elements—Beams	Underpinning Elements—Rocks
Open & Honest Communication	Pay & Benefits
Purpose, Mission & Values	Wellbeing
Leadership	Workspace
Management	
Job Design	
Learning	
Recognition	

Like bridging a stream, the whole Engagement Bridge™ doesn't have to be beautiful, complete and perfect before you can start to get people across it. Some organizations get great engagement with just a few—charities stand out as excelling on Mission and Purpose; people often go to work for them because they deeply believe in the cause—curing cancer or saving pandas. This can create great engagement just from Mission and Purpose alone, but if they work on some of the rest of the Bridge, they'll get an even more successful, effective and durable culture.

Engagement is Never Complete

You don't have to get everything right before you start seeing positive changes in engagement. Nothing here will ever be perfect; making progress is what is important.

While we've thought carefully about the order and placement of elements in the Bridge™, it's important not to take the placings too literally. Although recognition appears at the top, it is not intended to be the "cherry on top." For many companies, it is essential and, because it's also quite straightforward, many companies might actually start with it. Leadership and Management, which appear as smaller elements of the Bridge™, are not half as important as Purpose, Mission & Values—we show them on one line to indicate how interconnected they are.

Finally, you don't start at the top and work down or on the left and work across—you set your own direction and order. Our guidance is to start where you can make a quick impact—*the enemy of progress is inertia.*

Unpacking the Bridge™

While the Bridge™ has 10 elements, we think of them in five parts.

Open & Honest Communication

Creating a culture of open and honest communication is so important that we call it the foundation of the Engagement Bridge™. In fact, in all of the 2,000 companies we've worked with, we haven't found one that has had success in engagement and hasn't made a significant effort in this area.

The reason that open and honest communication is so important is that it is so closely linked to *employee trust*. Without trust, it's very hard to imagine an engaged culture where people voluntarily put the company, and its mission and purpose, first.

Purpose, Mission & Values

With a baseline of honesty and transparency established, having a clear direction and purpose plus a consistent way of behaving drives employee engagement. There is something deeply human about the need to feel part of something bigger than yourself—something that feels worthwhile, something that feels purposeful and worth the sacrifice of your time. Getting paid and creating money for shareholders simply isn't enough for the vast majority of people to feel this connection. They need more.

Ford wants to "*go further to make our cars better, our employees happier and our planet a better place to be.*" Atlassian wants "*to unleash the potential in every team and help advance humanity through the power of software.*" For Google, it's "*to organize the world's information and make it universally accessible and useful.*" They're all different, but they all provide a sense of meaning and purpose for employees to get behind.

Leadership and Management

These are separate elements of the Bridge™, but we show them together on a single line to emphasize the link between them. To some extent, Leadership is what the company *says* it will do, while Management is what the company actually *does*. The CEO has to make sure that management keeps the promises that the leader makes.

If you have leaders who espouse great customer service, dedication to innovation and treating people fairly, but local management who don't feel connected, empowered or driven to deliver that, then you'll have an *inauthentic culture*. The same goes for process and procedures: If the wall says *"Delight your customer,"* but the process manual or computer is always saying *"no,"* then again, your culture is inauthentic and your staff will spot this in a second. That's why we present these elements together: because they are so closely intertwined.

Job Design, Learning and Recognition

These three elements are hyper-connected because we know that the best-designed jobs, the most successful and engaging roles, have recognition (and visibility) and learning (and development) built into them right from the start. A boring job where you have no meaningful output, no sense of achievement, and no one seeming to notice if you do it or not is not made better by sticking a recognition program and a subscription to an e-learning platform on the side of it.

Fundamentally, to be able to be engaged, someone has to be in a job that has some degree of autonomy and accountability, and produces meaningful results that are seen and recognized. And any job will become disengaging if it does not develop and progress over time.

Pay & Benefits, Workspace, and Wellbeing

These final three elements are different because they are your underpinning elements—underpinning your engagement strategy. They are not the same as the connecting elements that run across, since you cannot engage your workforce with these elements alone.

They remain hugely important. If these elements in your strategy are lacking, then your bridge will be built on unstable ground; the complete absence of them will prevent progress on engagement completely. Pay, in particular, can be an enormous disengager of your people, especially if they perceive it as dealt with unfairly. With pressures on pay in many industries, getting this right can be a minefield.

Many organizations at the start of their employee engagement journeys choose to start with a simple new employee perk or benefit to act as an olive branch with the workforce. The key to success is to make sure you use this as a starting point and not an end in itself.

Company Culture is the Output of the Bridge™

We're often asked how the Bridge™ links to culture or why company culture isn't an element of the Bridge™ itself. Company culture is the output of your collective actions (or inactions). The Bridge™ shows your inputs. **You can change culture, but you only change it by making changes to the inputs**—and they are the elements of the Bridge™.

Everything on the Bridge™ is something that you can control. You can choose to invest time and resources in any of the elements of the Bridge™, and that investment, if directed well, will improve the connection you have between your organization and your employees.

It's important to think about the culture you *have* and the culture you *want* as you start building your bridge and developing your organization. Directing a company's culture is about so much more than writing down company values.

Actions Make Company Culture, Not Words

How your company behaves, recruits, makes decisions, operates, makes choices, through the actions of your leaders and managers: That's what forms your culture.

There is no better place to start than here, and no better time to start than now. In the chapters that follow, we'll walk you through the 10 elements of the Engagement Bridge™ model, give you practical tips on how to get started and share the inspirational stories or "plays" of the rebel companies in this playbook. As you read, think about who will help you in your organization, who your fellow rebels will be and who can join you in your *"rebelution."* Get them to read this book with you, get them to join you and help you.

And remember, **the way we treat people at work has failed**. It has resulted in a world where only 30% of people are engaged at work and half of us are looking for a new job.

If this book seems judgmental about the way we work at the moment, it's because we are failing and we have to change—we have to rebel against the status quo.

Let's get to it!

3

Open & Honest Communication

Chapter Objectives

In this chapter, we will:

- Discuss the link between open and honest communication and trust.
- Be honest about the role that HR has had in creating mistrust through under-communicating.
- Understand that a key goal should be a culture where staff trust leadership enough to speak up.

Key Points

- Open and honest communication is the foundation of employee engagement because of its link with trust.
- This will take work and commitment at all levels of management.
- To build a high-trust culture, you have to make room for dissent, disagreement and diversity of opinion.
- The best companies develop cultures of lateral transparency across the company between peers and departments.

Introduction

The foundation of the Engagement Bridge™ is Open & Honest Communication. You can make good progress in engagement without being a master of every element, but we haven't seen any companies do well at employee engagement that did not have real momentum and focus on their open and honest communication strategy.

No One Trusts Us When We Lie

A lack of trust is the issue at the heart of employee disengagement, and it's caused by the fact that we persistently lie to each other at work. We've been doing this for so long and it's so entrenched that most of the time, we barely notice we're doing it.

We start the practice of telling lies about work in our schools and colleges when we train young students in *interview skills*. "Interview skills" is educational code for lying—lying by presenting a version of yourself that is not true, not really you and not really your whole self. Companies also lie at interviews, from the recruitment ads to the promises of perfect roles we know aren't real. With both sides working so hard to cover up the truth, is it any wonder that so many jobs end after 18 months?

We continue lying under the guise of *professionalism:* a set of behaviors that adheres to some unwritten code of how we think we should behave at work that is not the real us.

We lie with concepts such as *permanent jobs* when, of course, there is no such thing, and then lie throughout the rest of the employment relationship with half-truths, withheld information and saying one thing when we mean another. We tell ourselves that we're doing this to "protect our employees," but the end result is simply disengagement through lack of trust.

We Need to Stop the Lies Now

Lying to our staff, telling half-truths, withholding information and compulsive under-communication destroys trust in organizations. It creates an "us and them" culture and sabotages any possibility of employee engagement. If you're serious about employee engagement, you need to stop the lies and build trust instead.

This chapter is dedicated to the radical, revolutionary, rebellious idea of telling the truth, defaulting to transparency, and being open and honest—just like our parents told us to do when we were kids.

The Trust Issue

The Edelman Trust Barometer has been measuring the state of trust in business, media, non-governmental organizations (NGOs) and government since 1990. In 2016, Edelman examined the state of trust between employers and employees for the first time and found that trust in the organization decreases as you go lower down the hierarchy:

- 64% of executives trust their companies
- 51% of managers trust their companies
- 48% of what Edelman called "rank and file" employees trust their companies

The blame goes to a simple lack of basics and of doing what you promise. Edelman recommends: "Be honest. Do what you say you'll do. Admit when you're wrong. Provide context. And listen. It's far easier to trust a human being with a face, name, and values than a title on a business card."

We have to be really honest with ourselves: HR departments should take a lot of the blame, followed by their partner-in-crime, the legal department. They expend huge amounts of an organization's relationship capital with its staff on attempting not to get sued. Policies are made complex with rules, documents are written as if all employees are out to cheat us, contractual clauses are written with a one-sided employer-friendly view, and—perhaps most importantly—untruths and half-truths are told in employee communications.

The tragedy is that much of this relationship capital is squandered in protecting the organization from theoretical risk that never happens and, if it did, wouldn't have cost much anyway.

> *"Many of us in HR go to work every day thinking all of our staff are out to sue us all the time. So we invent all these rules and policies. Couldn't we try something different? Maybe our people wouldn't sue us so much if we didn't piss them off with the lies?"*
>
> —Patty McCord,
> Former Chief Talent Officer at Netflix and author of Powerful

In an effort to spare the embarrassment of someone who has left, or to comply with a hastily written settlement agreement, the reason for a job termination is rarely shared. This leaves a void that fear and cynicism fills. People remember *"that nice guy who was just fired for no good reason—his face didn't fit,"* when the reality was often very different. Fear and suspicion always fill an information vacuum.

When I was CEO at Reward Gateway, I had a policy that we never sign away our right to explain why someone left in a settlement agreement or any other contract. Every time you cover up the true reasons for someone leaving your organization, you destroy trust with your people, and that trust is just too hard to earn and too valuable to lose.

The Crime of Under-communicating

Under-communicating also erodes trust. You know the story: Sales aren't where you hoped they'd be or you've got retention problems, but if you tell everyone, it will worry them and they will fear for their jobs. You keep it quiet until the axe drops and you make the layoffs instead.

When it comes to talking honestly and openly, Richard Plepler, CEO of HBO, has a saying: *"The building knows the truth."* Everyone knows the problems in the business because they sit next to the sales team who missed their goals, see the worried look on managers' faces and notice the closed-door meetings.

> *"If you want people to make the same decisions that you would make, but in a more scalable way, you have to give them the same information you have."*
>
> —Keith Rabois,
> Investor at PayPal, LinkedIn and Square

While working for a team that missed its targets is disappointing, having that information means your people can start becoming part of the solution. But too many people work in companies that miss their targets *and* keep employees in the dark or lie to them. That's where trust collapses, fear comes in and disengagement happens.

Communicating Means Listening as Well as Speaking

As I talk to CEOs and HR leaders, it's remarkable just how many of them share their fear of not hearing the truth from the front line—of people not speaking up. But very few leaders make enough real effort to build a culture where people speak up freely, believing it will occur magically by itself. It doesn't. The truth is it takes enormous, constant effort to build an atmosphere where you can hear the truth.

The problem is in the hierarchy. The power resides at the top, while all the information resides at the bottom. Sidney Yoshida quantified this in his 1989 landmark study, "The Iceberg of Ignorance,"[1] where he found that only 4% of an organization's front-line problems are known by top management, 9% by middle management, 74% by managers and 100% by employees.

Iceberg of Ignorance

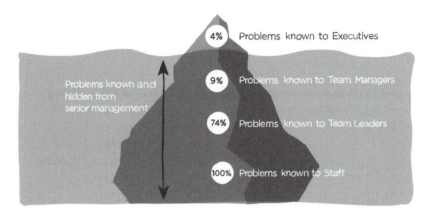

If we are to improve this information flow, we need to attack it from multiple angles. At the top, we need to help executives understand where the information is, and coach and develop them in ways to discover that information in a non-threatening way. This includes developing an approach that will encourage junior staff to speak up to them and also installing mechanisms and technology that allow staff to do this anonymously when they want or need to.

In the middle, we need to create an environment where managers don't feel they have to show perfection up the chain

[1]Sidney Yoshida, first presented at the International Quality Symposium, Mexico City, Mexico, 1989.

and hide dysfunction. I've always asked my direct reports for complete honesty and have told them that if they tell me everything is perfect in their department, I'll assume they are lying, ignorant or just have low standards.

At the front line, we need to enable, encourage and reward people who speak up and make sure that they are free from fear of judgment or reprisal. Executives need to respond to all feedback that's given—it is hard to get, and it's critical to show encouragement to staff brave enough to give it.

In Practice

Key Outcomes Rebels Strive For

When we look at organizations that have made significant headway toward a culture of open and honest communication, we see three key benefits.

Improved Trust   The most visible and measurable benefit is improved trust between colleagues, between colleagues and managers, and between colleagues and the company's leadership.

Better Alignment to Goals   Getting more of our staff to row in the same direction remains a key business challenge. Improvements in how businesses communicate lead to more staff who understand and trust company strategy on a sufficiently detailed basis to inform their own daily decision-making.

Lower-risk Decision-making   A culture of openness and transparency is what improves decision-making and lowers risk, because people in charge of the decision can rely on the fact that their colleagues speak up, debate and give their views. It is in these radically open cultures that the best thinking develops.

Key Rebel Behaviors

We've found companies crack the open and honest communications code in five key ways:

1. **Default to transparency**
   Rebels make everything open, visible and public unless something absolutely has to be made private or closed to a team, group or department. They use open messaging technology like Slack, collaborate in open systems like Google Docs, and have an understanding that secrecy should be questioned and challenged.

   > *"Be as open with your people as you can, as early as you can. Employees are much more likely to go to bat for something they understand."*
   > —Helen Craik,
   > Reward Gateway Co-founder and architect of the
   > early culture

2. **Explain why**
   Rebels communicate company decisions and strategy in a unique and highly effective way. They place significant emphasis on explaining the "*why*," so the reason and thinking behind key decisions comes before getting into the "*how*."

3. **Make room for dissent, disagreement and diversity of opinion**
   Rebels listen constantly. They value diversity of opinion and create teams that include people with different perspectives. They create multiple channels for employees to share their views, ideas, and concerns to leadership on a routine, everyday basis.

4. **Communicate continuously with warmth and emotion**
   Rebels communicate constantly using a wide variety of channels. They repeat key messages and there is an assumption, a habit, that communication is a job never done. They communicate with rich, human stories, building relationships and constantly asking, "*How will people feel when they hear or read this?*"

5. **Invest in** *lateral transparency*

   Rebels create a culture where peers are open and honest with each other, departments feel safe in being candid, and there is a high degree of *lateral transparency* in the business. They encourage relationships between people across teams with social communication, social recognition and open directory tools. They promote a culture that allows constant feedback and improvement to occur between people, something that author Kim Scott calls "*building a culture of radical candor.*"[2]

Making a Start

The cost of improving transparency is almost zero in cash terms, but requires an ongoing dialogue between management and staff, a real commitment from leadership, and the courage to disrupt years of established HR and company communications practice.

Communicate from the Heart—Write Like You're Talking to One Person Think about how each department will feel when they read a piece of company communication. Think about their questions and objectives in advance and head these off: Include them right in the document in a Q&A section. Never shy away from hard questions—where possible, get some outspoken employees to help you expose hard questions early; they're always better out in the open. If you're announcing something that isn't in line with a previous announcement, pull that thread yourself by adding a question, such as "Doesn't this contradict what we said last quarter?" Be honest in every response. Find some examples at **rg.co/intcomms**.

Iterate and Get Input, but Don't Compromise to Get Consensus Compromise is the enemy of clarity. So is writing by committee. Just because you ask for comments and opinion doesn't mean you should adopt them. Some of the worst, most confusing documents are created when eight people are asked to

---

[2] See rg.co/kimscott

review something, everyone adds a bit and then the author generally accepts all comments for fear of offending someone. What results is a document unidentifiable to the author, unintelligible to the reader and lacking any ownership.

Feedback from a small group of real front-line employees is infinitely better than asking what all the leadership team think, so try to build a small group of trusted people who understand your workforce and are unafraid to speak up.

Use Every Channel You Can; Repeat, Repeat, Repeat

Our attention is heavily fragmented now—that's just reality. You need to accept that no single channel will reach everyone. Maybe no single channel will even reach 20% of people, but five channels added together might reach 60%, and that's a great place to start.

Work to overcome your fear or dislike of social media channels like Facebook, Snapchat and Instagram—this is where the eyes and ears of your people are. Use these channels to signpost articles from your intranet and share whole articles and stories where confidentiality allows. Repeat communications multiple times across channels. Remember: *"The greatest enemy of communication is the illusion that it has occurred."*[3]

THE PLAYS

Transparent Approach to Communicating Salaries: *Buffer*

Situation

Social media company Buffer is known for its radical approach to communication and transparency, doing something unprecedented by sharing salaries of all 71 employees, posting them on a public website for all the world to see. And not

---

[3]Originally written as "The great enemy of communication, we find, is the illusion of it. We have talked enough; but we have not listened," in 1950 in the *Fortune* magazine article "Is Anybody Listening?" by William H. Whyte. Told to Glenn by Anne Allen at Xero.

just salaries, but its customer pricing model, revenues, equity grants, and even money spent on retreats and perks. Why, why would a company take this bold and very visible approach?

To answer this question, you have to look at one of their 10 values, **_default to transparency_**, which addresses transparency with two groups. The first is with employees, and talks about sharing thoughts immediately and with honesty. As CEO Joel Gascoigne says, the reason is that "transparency breeds trust, and trust is the foundation of great teamwork."[4] The second is with customers, using transparent communication as a tool to help others. "Taking the extra step and making it public as well is extending that trust to a different set of people—role modelling it to customers and blog readers and prospective team members," says Gascoigne.

Play

Buffer's transparent approach to sharing salaries has evolved and become more robust as the company has grown. It began by sharing salaries with the original 10 employees, explaining the rationale and formula behind each figure. After internal conversations, the company took the next step and shared salaries externally. As Gascoigne wrote at the time, "We hope this might help other companies think about how to decide salaries, and will open us up to feedback from the community."

The approach Buffer uses and shares is its "transparent salary formula." Now in its third version, the formula has evolved based on feedback received both internally and externally. Beginning with the objective of developing salaries that provide a good standard of living, the formula takes into account the market value of the job, the employee's location and their experience level. As Gascoigne says, transparent pay "gives employees one less thing to worry or gossip about and introduces a level of fairness." To read more about this, go to **rg.co/buffersalaries**.

---

[4]For a video interview with Joel visit rg.co/joelgascoigne

The company has seen real benefits to this transparent approach; starting, when it first went live, with a 50% increase in job applicants. It's also acted as a way to share a bit of Buffer's culture very early in the process with applicants, so they're quickly able to decide whether Buffer's unique values feel like the right fit. Other ways it's helped relate back to the objective of helping others, "providing a blueprint for others to use as they eradicate inequalities in pay, with nowhere to hide in this transparent environment," says Courtney Seiter, Director of People.

In Practice

- This may seem a bit rebellious for some companies, but there are still steps you can take, no matter how small, to be more transparent in the communication of salaries. Whether it's communicating your pay philosophy, pay practices or salary ranges, take action to be more transparent with your employees.

Showing and Telling to Keep Communication Open: *Wistia*

Situation

When Wistia, an internet video hosting company, was a seven-person company, it began a tradition of weekly standup meetings. The meetings were a vehicle for keeping the lines of communication open among the small team, so everyone was informed about what they'd done and learned each week. As the team grew to 100, though, the company faced the challenge of keeping this important tradition alive. Could the standup meetings still work, or should the tradition be sidelined?

In the end, the team decided that the tradition of this vital communication vehicle was too important to give up on, so they evolved it to work for their new workforce. "These meetings are critical to our business as it creates important cultural moments where connections occur and innovation begins," says founder and CEO Chris Savage.[5]

Play

Wistia's new format is called "Show and Tell," and is a weekly 30-minute all-hands meeting. The format is simple: Anyone can share a 5-minute (or less) presentation; people share creative ideas, projects and customer interactions; and last but not least, everyone cheers for everyone else. Much like the child's game, where children bring in and share their prized possessions, employees get that same excited feeling by proudly sharing what they've accomplished.

"As our company's grown, meetings have become extremely focused and no-nonsense, and everyone is busy with their weekly tasks. But it's crucial to stay excited about having innovative, unexpected ideas. That's how teammates stay motivated to build, plan, design, write, produce and work in original ways. That's how companies grow," says Savage.

The results have been that team members are more connected and more honest, sharing both good and bad to make the company and the product better with every passing Show and Tell.

In Practice

- Create your own version of the "Show and Tell" game to help your workforce gain insights into what is happening in the business around them and to open up the lines of communication.

---

[5]For a video interview with Chris visit rg.co/chrissavage

Revolutionize Teamwork With a "Get to Know Me" Guide for Every Member of Staff: *BetterCloud*

Situation

When David Politis, founder and CEO of BetterCloud, attended the *New York Times* "New Work Summit" conference, he was inspired by a session hosted by Adam Bryant, a columnist for the *New York Times*. Bryant's session, titled "The CEO's User Manual," talked about the importance of CEOs creating a "how-to-work-with me" guide to be given to their workforce to help employees understand how best to work with them and gain their trust.

"What a brilliant idea—it makes you kick yourself and wonder, why didn't I think of doing that?" says Politis. He embraced the concept so much that he invited his entire workforce to create their own guides. As Politis explains, "Why should it be limited to learning how to work with the CEO only? The learning curve seems to be even more pronounced in intra- and inter-team interactions, which happen a lot more on a daily basis than interactions with me do. So I took it one step further: I decided to have the whole company create user manuals."

This approach and tool has had a positive impact on team members working together more effectively, with increased trust and cooperation, leading to stronger working relationships.

Play

The how-to-work-with me guide outlines what you like, what you don't like and how you work best. As Politis says, "It's a 'cheat sheet' of sorts, giving colleagues a way to quickly and efficiently learn about each other, which in turn allows them to work together more effectively."

Politis introduced the concept at a company meeting, explaining why he felt the guide was valuable and sharing his with employees. He then asked everyone to take out their laptops and begin an exercise to create their own guides. "I don't think we've ever had a period of time where every person in the company was typing at the same time—they were so absorbed that nobody was talking or looking up; everyone was just furiously typing away. But the coolest part of it all was when we finished and people went back to their desks: I noticed everyone was in the Shared Drive folder and avidly reading each other's user manuals, curious to learn more," says Politis.

The guides have become a part of the company, providing a simple tool to encourage conversations about communication styles and learn more about each other. They've led to a more productive, open and transparent environment.

In Practice

- Create your own version of "how-to-work-with me" guides at your company, even if only at the leadership team level initially. They'll help bridge the employee trust gap by presenting leaders in an open, honest and transparent way. See examples on **rg.co/guidetome**.

Communicating and Leading a Business Through Challenging Times: *GM Holden Ltd*

Situation

It was 2013, and Holden, one of Australia's largest car manufacturers, was faced with a challenging situation, one putting both the business and employee engagement to the test. After being told the plant would be closing in four years, the leadership had to make some difficult decisions: when and what to tell their employees, and how to manage the business for the remaining years.

The strategy and approach the leadership team developed is a stellar example of employee engagement at its best, which is even more amazing given their situation. Where some companies would focus on winding down the business, Holden made the decision to ramp up and focus on its people. According to Jamie Getgood, HR Director, "If all we do as a leadership team is simply shrink the business, we will have failed our people and our customers. Our people genuinely care for each other, and our last car will be the best we ever built."[6]

Play

Holden's new focus on its people was comprehensive and best in class, so much so that other companies facing similar challenges began to solicit the company's assistance. It involved the following:

- **Transparent communication** by removing the veil of secrecy that had existed in the past, creating a transparent and two-way approach. This began with sharing the news of the plant closure immediately, and continued throughout the transition period, treating employees with respect and trust.
- **Improved employee focus** by putting money and effort into improving the employee experience. Whether this involved maintaining the gardens, upgrading bathrooms, or having site-wide activities and events (e.g. classic car days, family days, charity events), Holden showed employees that the company cared for them in many ways.
- **New methods of connection** by having daily production walks by the leadership team to stay close/connected to employees at this critical time, helping them understand and react to the needs of the business and employees.
- **Increased transition support** by using a three-phase approach to "support and give employees confidence,

---

[6]For a video interview with Jamie, visit rg.co/jamiegetgood

preparing them for their next journey," says Getgood. Phase One helped employees understand themselves, Phase Two helped them explore further career opportunities and Phase Three provided outplacement services. It's been a huge success, with 82% of employees participating in the program.

With these new initiatives, Holden spent more on its people over the final four years than in the previous 10. Did it make a difference? Absolutely, yes! The company's workplace-of-choice metrics, which included engagement, increased a staggering 20 to 30%; attendance improved; processes improved; and the quality of the cars built in the facility attained world-class standards. Holden's workforce rallied around the business to truly support it and to leave with their heads held high, being proud of what they had accomplished and done during this challenging period.

In Practice

- Employee engagement can and should happen at all times, both good and bad, because it can help support and drive your business whatever the situation.

- Look for opportunities to engage with your employees as often and as soon as possible. Their input is valuable and can help improve business operations.

Bringing all the Ingredients Together to Create Engagement: *Krispy Kreme Australia*

Situation

Krispy Kreme, the doughnut and coffeehouse chain, is passionate about delivering delicious tastes and connecting both customers and employees with moments of happiness. Key to this is engaging and connecting with its workforce, and aligning with values that focus on creating situations and destinations that bring people together.

The company felt a key way to create this connection was through communication, but hadn't found a scalable approach that would also align employees with business goals and company values. Over the years, it had used a variety of approaches and media to communicate with its 850 employees in multiple locations, but the leadership felt important messages weren't reaching all employees. "Our intention was to give people exposure to the business beyond what they see every day, and context for how their role fits into the bigger picture. We believed this would drive engagement and showcase how great a company Krispy Kreme is to work for," says Sally Park, Head of People for Krispy Kreme Australia.[7]

The result has been to create an online communications hub, one that shares information in an open, honest and transparent way. "This has been the beginning of our journey to open up how and when we communicate to our workforce. It gives us a tool to improve engagement, trust and connection with our people today and in the future," says Park.

Play

Krispy Kreme developed a centralized communications platform that they named "KK Mixer". The hub keeps employees connected to Krispy Kreme's culture and business goals by featuring regular updates on what's going on in the business, such as new promotions, sales results, community involvement and even the number of doughnuts made (very important to know!). The hub also hosts other tools, such as benefits and recognition, so all employees can easily access them.

A regular feature of the platform is the updates from Australia's CEO Andrew McGuigan and his heads of department. These help employees understand what's going on at the

[7]For a video interview with Sally, visit rg.co/sallypark

company by sharing results, progress and even challenges, strengthening their connection to the business and strategy.

"With the introduction of KK Mixer, we've transitioned our HR communications to a branded, culture-driven platform that employees love engaging with," Park says, "and as they're engaging with the platform, they're learning more. About the company, and about how they can make it a better place to work. We will continue to learn, too, while we continue to evolve the KK Mixer to meet the changing needs of our business."

In Practice

- Bring your communication material together in one place to make it easier for your workforce and to show them your commitment to an open and transparent approach to communication.
- Give your employee communications the same care and attention as you do your customer communications. This shows employees your commitment to creating the best employee experience possible.

Giving Your Employees a Seat at the Table: *HSBC*

Situation

When Stuart Gulliver became Group CEO of HSBC in 2011, he recognized that the international bank needed to make a cultural shift, setting a new direction for the business and for how its global workforce of 230,000 employees communicated and worked together. According to Pierre Goad, Group Head of Communications, "We needed to look at what went wrong back in the 'noughties,' creating the right environment for our people to speak up about what was going on in the company, taking shared responsibility for creating change."[8]

This objective laid the path for a more progressive approach to HSBC's communication strategy, and to the development of the "HSBC Exchange" program. This program has not only set the standard in the industry for an open and transparent approach to communication, but has had a profound and positive impact at HSBC, including a 10–20 percentage point positive differential on key sentiment metrics between those who have attended an exchange meeting and those who haven't.

Play

HSBC Exchange, otherwise known as the "shut up and listen" program, was launched with the aim of helping to move communication from being one-way and not very "free-flowing" to a situation where multiple conversations could happen in every direction—up, down and peer-to-peer. It's a unique forum that helps employees share their thoughts and views freely, and then cascades this information from the bottom to the top. It has set the scene for a new type of communication at HSBC, one that encourages and creates an environment where employees can not only speak up but feel it's their responsibility to do so.

There are three simple rules for Exchange meetings: The manager does not talk but just listens, there is no agenda, and the time belongs to the employees. Topics could be on the food served in the canteen, a local process or the big issues that affect the company—employees make the decision. "In the first meetings, discussions centered around problems or complaints, which is what you'd expect as they're things employees needed to get off their chests. But over time, the discussions and topics have become broader—some are about customers, others about how to make our products better or improve customer service, while others are about how employees can develop their careers," says Goad.

---

[8]For a video interview with Pierre, visit rg.co/pierregoad

HSBC had a few challenges at the start of the program. Many managers found the art of being quiet uncomfortable and confusing, but they quickly realized the value of this approach and the results they achieved. Many employees did not know how to participate in this type of meeting. "For the first 10 minutes, employees often sat in silence. However, now that the meetings have become more business as usual, the conversations flow naturally and employees understand and appreciate their role and their voice," says Goad.

Important to the success of this program is that HSBC did not set a fixed schedule for when the meetings should take place, and did not force managers to conduct them. Instead, they let the results speak for themselves, with people quickly realizing their value, which encouraged them to take place organically. HSBC have truly created a "speak up" culture, giving all 230,000 employees a seat at the table where conversations can happen and changes can be made.

In Practice

- Find ways to create forums for your employees to truly speak up— it benefits both employees and the company.
- Don't feel you have to push and force change; often letting the results speak for themselves will be enough for your workforce to embrace it.

4

Purpose, Mission & Values

Chapter Objectives

In this chapter, we will:

- Examine why clearly developed Purpose, Mission & Values (PMV) is critical to engagement.
- Discuss how an inspiring mission is key for staff to get behind.
- Look at how documenting and embedding company values can play a key role in guiding behavior.

Key Points

- Companies need an inspirational and authentic mission and livable values that support and drive the business and employees.
- Clear and well-communicated PMV inspires employees, connects customers and creates alignment.
- PMV has to be more than just words: It must be lived. Misalignment between words and actions is inauthentic, and can be a key disengager.
- Genuinely embedding values in your organization will have a dramatic effect, so make sure they are the right ones. It takes time, but is hugely valuable, so get started now.

Introduction

In the last chapter, we talked about the importance of open and honest communication, explaining it was a foundation of employee engagement. If communication gives you a foundation on which to build an engaged culture, Purpose, Mission & Values (PMV) gives your culture both direction and a way of working to get there.

Let's start by defining some key terms, showing how they each answer a key question:

- **Mission**—*What* big goal or outcome is your organization committed to?
- **Purpose**—*Why* does that goal have to be achieved? Who benefits?
- **Values**—*How* will your company behave to make that happen?

Don't obsess about mission vs. purpose or worry about precise definitions. Just get working on what your organization is here to do, why that matters and how you will do that.

Here's an example, using Reward Gateway's PMV.[1]

Mission (What)	Purpose (Why)	Values (How)
To make the world a better place to work.	We believe people deserve great jobs because there is something deeply human about meaningful work. We believe engaged employees build better, stronger, more successful organizations.	Delight your customer. Be human. Think global. Push the boundaries. Speak up. Own it. Love your job. Work hard.

---

[1]Get more details and a description of these values from **rg.co/culturebook**.

Mission Matters

A well-developed, clearly articulated and inspiring mission will:

- Give employees something bigger and more meaningful to work toward, which has a proven positive impact on results.[2]
- Let customers connect with you on a deeper level.
- Support long-term decision-making, aligning everyone with a clear common goal.

Believing Work has Meaning and Purpose Helps Teachers Cope with Stress Better, Directly Improving Performance

Teaching is a profession with high burnout rates—along with emergency responders, nuclear power plant operators and doctors. Adam Grant, a professor at Wharton whose research focuses on generosity, motivation and meaningful work, studied the relationship between stress and burnout and the extent to which teachers felt their jobs really made a difference.

He found that teachers who believed in their purpose, who really felt that their actions had a meaningful impact on students' lives, were significantly better able to handle their job and avoid burnouts. In his words,

> *"They were better able to cope with job stressors when they knew how much impact they were having on students. Because their work made a difference, it was worth putting up with long hours of grading and administrative red tape and angry parents."*
> —Adam Grant,
> Professor at Wharton, author of Originals and Give and Take

---

[2]Adam Grant studied the link between mission, productivity and success, and found a 4× increase in the results of telemarketers when they were connected to a mission. See **rg.co/adamgrant**.

An inspiring and well-defined mission, in isolation, doesn't make for an engaged company culture, but when you stack up your values, mission, operating processes and employer brand, you're starting to build the narrative and the story of your organization.

One way you can do it is to write your company's obituary—think about how you would want your company to be remembered. Thinking about the end goal and how you want people to remember the business can help you define the behaviors that will get you there.

The Case for Company Values

If your mission is a signpost to why you are here, where you are going and what you're trying to do, your values should codify the behaviors you want to use to get there.

Done properly, this is one of the most strategic things you will ever do. While it's good practice to involve staff in developing these values, they should be signed off at the highest level: your CEO and the leadership team. This is essential for two key reasons:

1. It's going to take years of work, discipline and commitment to embed your values. You need your board to buy into this as a long-term process and also raise a flag if they think a business change is coming that could wrong-foot you or suggest you've chosen the wrong values.
2. If you embed them correctly and follow through, they will work: They will literally change how your organization behaves. That means you have to be sure that they're right or you'll have the whole organization singing the wrong tune and having a negative effect on business performance.

Designing or Changing Values

Depending on your situation and what you want to accomplish, you can (and should) design values in different ways. Consider carefully what you're trying to achieve, since values are powerful when they're correctly implemented.

Situation	Recommended Strategy
You have a good culture and you want to keep that culture as you grow.	Engage with staff to document what they already see in the business. When things are already good, harnessing your staff to do a grassroots-led project is powerful.
You aim to build on a successful past with a change of emphasis or an additional aspect.	Again, engage staff, but ask them to document what they see to either add an aspirational value or expand upon language in the values you have currently.
You need to fix a broken culture in an emergency.	Only when a culture is broken and you've had a scandal or real issues with business performance should you consider imposing new values from above. It's critical, though, to follow through ruthlessly—many existing employees may not live or want to live by those new values.[3]

Your values define your organization, so they should be unique to you and set you apart from others. One of the biggest criticisms employees have about company values is when they are seen as bland and like every other company.

With that in mind, let's look at three very different examples.

Slack, the team messaging company, is a fast growing startup. It was founded by four people who'd worked together for over a decade, giving them the confidence to write the values

---

[3]See **rg.co/emergencyvalues** for a story of how startup Zenefits did this after a compliance scandal.

they wanted in their business right from the start and to design a culture around those.

Based in Silicon Valley, Slack is at the center of the world's greatest war for engineering talent. In an effort to attract the right people, the company focused on creating values that were very *different* from other tech companies. The company is unique in showing a love for what it calls "useless liberal arts degrees" and it designed soft, emotional values to stand out.

> *"We didn't want the same values as everyone else—you know, 'Integrity, Respect,' stuff like that. I think they should be a given. Everyone has those. We wanted to really think about what was special at Slack, what was unique, what was just us."*
> —Stewart Butterfield, Founder & CEO at Slack

The result is a set of six values that, uniquely, are expressed as three sentences.

Slack's Six Values—Full Descriptions at rg.co/slack

1. **Empathy** as expressed through **courtesy**
2. **Craftsmanship** tempered with **playfulness**
3. **Thriving**, both in ourselves and others
   "both in ourselves and others" encompasses the 6th value—
   Solidarity

Slack shows authenticity by delivering these values through its product: Every time a user logs in, they see an inspirational quote from Brené Brown, a researcher and storyteller who focuses on shame and vulnerability.

Up the coast at **Amazon** in Seattle, 14 leadership principles take the place of corporate values. This itself makes a statement that it is leaders and leadership that Amazon values above all else.

Amazon's 14 Leadership Principles—Full descriptions at rg.co/amazon		
Customer Obsession	Hire and Develop the Best	Earn Trust
Ownership	Insist on the Highest Standards	Dive Deep
Invent and Simplify	Think Big	Have Backbone; Disagree and Commit
Are Right, A Lot	Bias for Action	Deliver Results
Learn and Be Curious	Frugality	

Each of the principles is evaluated carefully in Amazon's leadership recruitment process. Every candidate must be able to provide a detailed example that shows how they have lived each principle. If a single principle cannot be demonstrated or is not seen as being important to the candidate, the candidate is rejected, regardless of skills, experience or anything else. Amazon recruits and promotes exclusively on these leadership principles, making them absolutely core to the company.

Over at **Netflix**, values show behaviors the company wants from all of its staff. Nine company values helped power a unique culture through eight years of growth and evolution from a DVD mailing business to the world's leading video streaming platform, and now a content creator with original programming. Netflix added a 10th value, "*inclusion,*" in 2017, reflecting the company's new global customer base.

10 values at Netflix—Full descriptions at rg.co/netflix		
Judgment	Courage	Selflessness
Communication	Passion	Inclusion
Curiosity	Integrity	Impact
Innovation		

Founder Reed Hastings worked with Chief Talent Officer Patty McCord over 14 years to develop a unique culture that would give talented people more freedom and responsibility than they'd get at other organizations. Hastings and McCord envisaged an organization where, as the business grew and became more complex, they would hire better and better people into high-performing teams. They would resist the urge to bring in the safety of process and instead would give more and more freedom with accountability.

The cost of this was paying top-of-market salaries and having a zero-tolerance attitude toward *"adequate performance."* While neighboring startups focused on quirky perks and fancy offices, the line *"Adequate performance gets a generous severance package"* became a marker of the Netflix resolve to be better.

Each of these companies took a different approach to designing and implementing their values. They all have different business strategies, different workforces and completely different cultures, so it's right that they took an approach unique to them. Like fingerprints, unique to each of us, no two companies should have the same values, since they're the most powerful and authentic when they're one-of-a-kind.

In a crowded market for employees and customers, you must focus on *why* you are *different*, so think about what makes you special on an emotional level. Even if it means that some people will love those aspects and some will hate them, be brave enough to make them special and unique for yourself and your workforce.

Explain, Don't Just State, Your Values

Designing values is more than coming up with a set of words; the real time is spent on explaining what you really mean by those words and why they are relevant to your company. Your value descriptions are absolutely key—check out the weblinks above to see how Slack, Amazon and Netflix describe the behaviors they value.

Embedding Values is the Real Hard Work

All three of these companies are successful at least in part because they chose the values and mission that were distinct for them, and enacted those and made them real through all other parts of the Engagement Bridge™. That's key. If you fail to get your company to live the values through everyday actions, you'll join the ranks of the thousands of corporations that write one thing on the wall and then go do the opposite.[4]

Values Have to be Embedded

To be meaningful, you need to recruit against your values, reward against your values and promote against your values. You think you do? Do your pay review spreadsheets refer to performance against values? When you hire someone, do you score against values? When you promote someone, do you know in advance which values are essential to prove for that next level up?

---

[4]See **rg.co/enron** for a dramatic example.

Typical of companies with this sort of inauthentic culture is the continued employment of people who fail to live the values but are kept on because they hit their short-term performance targets. This is what's behind the *"No brilliant jerks"* policy that Netflix and other rebels have. The problem with brilliant jerks is that while they are performing personally, they're destroying the engagement and performance of the team around them, which everyone can see. The advice is clear: **Always fire brilliant jerks**.

> *"It only takes one asshole to destroy an entire team. Act quickly and remove any bad seeds no matter how good they are at writing software.*
> —Joe Stump, Tech Leader, Investor and
> ex-Lead Architect at Digg.com

In Practice

Key Outcomes Rebels Strive For

The best companies know the positive impact that purpose, mission and values can have on their organizations and they strive for the following.

Mission Motivation   Rebel companies have highly motivated workforces because they look to hire people who are or could get passionate about the mission. This gives them a huge head start on engagement.

Increased Productivity through Alignment   A 2016 report for Salesforce found that 86% of employees surveyed did not clearly understand their companies' strategies, which contributed to nearly half of employee time being spent on work that was not aligned to the strategy.

This shows that having a clearly defined mission and purpose doesn't just help productivity through engagement—it helps productivity through focus.

Attracting Customers A strong PMV provides a story that your customers can understand, can believe and buy into.

> *"When choosing a vendor, sometimes you can see the options are pretty similar. Sure, there are variations in approach around the edges, but you can see that either solution could do a good job. In those situations, I look to whether there is deeper substance to what the company is doing, do they seem to have a compelling strategy, a real purpose that we can get behind, be inspired by ourselves. Those companies are great; you feel a real momentum with them."*
>
> —Simon Naylor, Head of Group Benefits at
> Travis Perkins plc, UK

Key Rebel Behaviors

The best companies weave a strong code into their culture with meaningful PMV integrated across their business. They have inspirational and aspirational PMV that staff can get behind. Key ways they make this happen include:

1. **Communicate continually**
   Rebels never stop communicating. They find new and different ways to tell stories from different perspectives and in different formats. Their values are not just a poster on the wall; they run programs like value of the month, they prioritize in induction and they consistently look to share real-life stories where their values have been lived.

2. **Implement without reservation**
   Rebels unreservedly hire, promote, reward and fire according to their PMV. They don't waver from this and don't tolerate even high-performing people who fail to live the values.

3. **Refresh cautiously**
   Rebels walk a fine line of allowing values to mature gently, keeping consistency so they can be embedded, while also updating them when necessary because context or situations

change. They treat their values with respect, but know that cultures are alive and need progression.

4. **Reward and recognize**

   Rebels link their values deeply into employee recognition programs, ensuring there are tangible monetary and non-monetary incentives for living the values.

Making a Start

Dust off Your Old Values or Ask Staff to Create New Ones   If you have values that no one knows, get staff to review them. If you've never had values before, then ask staff to help create them. Using volunteers from a range of departments to discuss your company values and document what they see as the best behaviors in your business is a great way to start.

Download a workshop pack and resources to help you get started at **rg.co/valuesworkshop**.

Embed throughout Your HR Processes   Once you have the right values, talk to your HR team and managers about how to use and embed them in other HR processes. People will only take you seriously when you start doing this—when they become real and meaningful.

Spend time thinking about your values and how they apply to different roles. Does every member of staff need to exemplify every value? Are some values more important to some roles than others? How could you integrate them into assessment or performance development frameworks? How could they be used in promotion assessment and pay review?

Develop a Story or Model to Bring Your Values to Life   Finding a way that your values connect together can be a helpful way of explaining them and making them memorable.

At RG, we used a rocketship metaphor. The drawing and the story explains how our values link together to support our North Star value of "Delight your customers" that connects to our mission: "Let's make the world a better place to work." You can hear the story in a special video at **rg.co/rocketship**.

rg.co/rocketship

THE PLAYS

Designing Values to Fuel a New Phase of Growth: *Causeway Technologies*

Situation

Causeway Technologies, the world's leading supplier of software for the built environment, was ready to take the business to the next phase of its journey. To help achieve this, Causeway decided to "get the house in order" as Fiona Buchanan,[5] EVP Human Resources, says, which started with revisiting its vision and values.

The team embarked on an exercise to review and refresh their values, partnering with employees throughout. These efforts were backed by the company's new CEO, Colin Smith, who says, "It would be easy for me to come along and tell employees what the vision and values might be, but that doesn't get engagement, which I value above all. I wanted to get as many people as possible to contribute."

The result of this partnership has been a new vision and values that will truly drive and fuel the business for growth. Employees have said they've felt listened to and, as a result, are fully embracing them. Although they've just been rolled out, Buchanan has said they've already had a positive impact on engagement.

Play

There were two phases in the development of Causeway's new vision and values. The first had the executive team work together to create different versions/examples to share with employees. This helped with the second phase: conducting employee workshops to give employees a starting point for discussions. Buchanan says they were impressed with the outputs from workshops, since employees brought in a variety of fresh perspectives, viewpoints and themes. It also meant that employees embraced the new values, because they felt they'd had a role in developing them. Their new values are:

Be curious	Wow everyone	Own it	Be proud	Work together

Causeway next created a video using employee feedback and opinions drawn directly from the vision and values employee workshops. "The purpose was to illustrate the diversity of views,

---

[5]For a video interview with Fiona, visit rg.co/fionabuchanan

and remind staff how they contributed to the end result," says Buchanan. Watch the video at **rg.co/causeway,**

But the journey doesn't end here; in fact, it's just begun, according to Buchanan. Employees are now conducting workshops with teams, discussing what the new values mean to them and what they need to do to truly live and breathe them. This, along with everything else that's been done, will help Causeway and its aligned and engaged workforce go forward on the next step of their journey.

In Practice

- Collaborate with your workforce as you develop and refine your values, creating a sense of ownership and engagement that cannot be achieved by thrusting it upon them.
- Make sure that employees understand what values mean to them personally and their jobs, turning them from words into actions and behaviors.

Creating a Common Language Through Values: *Vocus Communications*

Situation

When Australian telecoms company Vocus Communications went through a merger and increased its workforce 10-fold, the company realized it needed to define a new identity by updating company values to ones that worked for *all* employees, regardless of which business they came from. It also opened up the opportunity to create new values that "tied people together," according to Denise Hanlon,[6] Head of Human Resources.

---

[6]For a video interview with Denise, visit rg.co/denisehanlon

Play

The result were four shiny new company values—ones that are both creative and honest. They were intended to bring people together, but also to be "practical, irreverent, a little bit cheeky—just like us," says Hanlon.

To create the values, "we took what was held dearly from each of the merged companies and put it into words," says Hanlon. "People were asked, 'What is most important to you?' 'Why did you join Vocus?' and 'What makes us different from the other telcos?' In the end, they represent what Vocus has been and what it wants to be." The new values are:

Clever company, no muppets	Have a crack	Don't screw the customer	Don't be a d!@khead

They've been widely accepted throughout the organization, with employees proudly sharing them on social media. They've also created a common language for employees, one that's used as they work together across the new teams. An example is the value of not being a "d!@khead," which gives employees a commonly acceptable word for calling each other out when they're not behaving according to the values. "We've created values that are more than words; they have their own energy, they are a call to action. They make a massive difference to the way we treat our customers and our employees. In a company created from many other companies over time, they are our True North," says Hanlon.

In Practice

- Use your values as a way to create a common and widely spoken language for your workforce.
- Don't be afraid to be a bit cheeky if it's right for your company.

Leading a Business Based on Your Values:
G Adventures

Situation

In the summer of 2008, Bruce Poon Tip,[7] founder of G Adventures, made the decision that if he was going to stay with the company and lead it to the next level, it needed a "cultural revolution." "I had to go back to the very beginning and figure out where we stood. I wanted to harness this all together," said says Poon Tip. He brought employees from around the world to a series of meetings, and set out to document the company's new set of core values.

"Many companies have documented their core values, but the employees don't pay any attention. The document sits in a drawer somewhere, or the list is too long to remember," says Poon Tip. The company wanted core values that would transcend cultures and be easy enough to understand, "no matter whether you were a cook on a truck for us in Africa or a horse stableman in Mongolia."

Play

The group agreed on five new values, consisting of only a few words:

Love	Lead	Embrace	Create	Do

They next set out to bring them to life. One way was by *getting employees talking about them*, integrating them into how employees think and act. An example is its annual company-wide values-based video competition, where employees make short movies about what the values mean to them. The videos are not only hilarious, outrageous and clever, but they get

---

[7]For a video interview with Bruce, visit rg.co/brucepoontip

employees talking about and working together to bring meaning to the words. Go to **rg.co/gadventures** to see them.

Another key part of its strategy is to *use values to guide
decisions*. An example is a business decision about the company's policy on customer deposits. Standard practice in the travel
industry, and a way that travel companies make money, is for
companies to keep the customer's deposit if the customer can-
cels a trip. A group of G Adventures employees asked whether
that was taking advantage of people's misfortune, pointing out
that it went against the value of "doing the right thing."

Poon Tip and the team decided the employees were right,
and came up with the revolutionary idea of a lifetime deposit,
meaning a customer doesn't lose a deposit but can apply it toward
a new trip, give it to someone else or donate it to G Adventure's
charity. This is a great example of values clearly showing both
customers and employees who they are, helping employees and
the business get to the next level.

In Practice

- Challenge your company to use your values to drive both business
  and people decisions, even when they're difficult ones.
- Encourage your staff to police your values and speak up when
  company decisions or behaviors aren't in line.

Re-energizing a Program with a Purpose: *LinkedIn*

Situation

LinkedIn wanted to create a program that gave employees time to
"focus on themselves, the company and the world," says Nina

McQueen,[8] VP Global Benefits & Employee Experience. In 2010, they put a program in place called Investment Day or "InDay" for short. To meet the needs of the company's growing workforce, which McQueen described as "lean, driven, quickly spreading and out of breath," InDay was intended to energize teams, giving them a day each month to invest in themselves and their community.

Over the years, as the company grew to more than 8,000 in 30 cities around the world, InDay, like many programs in a high-growth environment, became less visible and effective. Many new employees didn't fully understand what InDay meant or how it should be used. This had to change; the program had to be refreshed.

Play

In 2014, LinkedIn did just that, re-energizing and relaunching this important and meaningful tradition. To do this, the team went back to basics by rebranding and restructuring it, creating renewed excitement and engagement with the program. The new program had a new look and feel, with monthly themes to provide something employees could unite around and "reveal the essence of who we are as a company," says McQueen. Themes included giving back, relationships, learning, wellness and play.

The team also leveraged others, using fellow employees to help create energy and engagement with the program. Executives now play an active role in sponsoring monthly themes and participating in events alongside employees, and LinkedIn's 250-strong culture champions from around the globe help execute events locally.

Finally, to ensure new hires understand the program, LinkedIn hired a storyteller to create a video to tell the story of InDay's origin and purpose through interviews with employees. All of these actions have paid off, re-energizing and turning InDay back into one of the company's most treasured and appreciated traditions.

---

[8]For a video interview with Nina, visit rg.co/ninamcqueen

In Practice

- As your company grows or time passes, find ways your values-linked programs can evolve or be re-energized to keep them alive. Don't think you have to start over or "throw in the towel."

- Consider ways your programs can create purpose, meaning, connection and collaboration among and between employees.

Changing Your Values as Your Company Becomes a "Teenager": *CarTrawler*

Situation

CarTrawler, the world's leading B2B travel technology platform, had values any company would be proud of. They were far from ordinary; in fact, they encapsulated the key attributes that made the company special. However, as the company grew, moving from being an infant to a teenager, as Gillian French,[9] Chief People Officer, explained, the company realized a change was needed to "grow up" and support the emerging business.

"We asked ourselves, are our values serving us well, or do they need to change to be able to handle our further growth?" says French. The decision was made to change them, launching the values alongside newly created purpose and mission statements to send a message about the new stage of the business's "life."

Play

In January 2017, the five new values were launched to replace the original four that had valiantly served the company's rapid growth until that point. They're united through the acronym HOPES, which is apt, given CarTrawler's forward-thinking attitude.

---

[9]For a video interview with Gillian, visit rg.co/gillianfrench

Value	Explanation
Humility	Humility replaced the original value of Irreverence, which reflected the desire to retain a fearless and informal way of conducting themselves. As the company grew, Humility was chosen to encapsulate both the feeling Irreverence brought and the modesty required for continued success.
Ownership	Ownership was added because it's imperative in a company of CarTrawler's size. It emphasizes the need to take ownership of a situation, using the mentality of constant improvement and owning it until completed.
Passion for improvement	This replaces Restless Satisfaction, which revolved around the drive to constantly strive to do things better. Although valued, as the company got bigger, it was felt that the old value was tripping people up, and it was more important to commit to completion.
Enthusiasm	Guiding a startup on a journey to a company of more than 500 employees is not possible without the belief and enthusiasm of its people. The infectious energy and startup passion that dominated its early years remained a key feature of CarTrawler's personality.
Smart Collaboration	Collaboration was an original value, but as the company grew it became clear that the old manner of collaborating wasn't working; in fact, it was hampering development. "Smart collaboration" encourages employees to deploy autonomy in their day-to-day tasks.

CarTrawler has shown the importance of balancing what makes you special at the start with what will support you as you continue to grow. The company values have truly evolved, and have helped and will continue to help the company as it moves not only from infant to teenager but from teenager to adult.

In Practice

- Keep in mind that as your business changes, your values have to change. Have them keep pace with change and they will continue to drive and support your business.

- Find ways to unify your values with something meaningful and memorable, such as the acronym used in this play.

A Purpose-Driven Approach to Volunteering: *Discovery Communications*

Situation

Discovery Communications, the broadcaster behind the Discovery Channel, TLC and Animal Planet channels, is dedicated not only to entertaining but inspiring, harnessing the power of its brands and businesses, and offering employees opportunities to give back to the world. With this in mind, the team decided to develop a range of global programs so the workforce, no matter where they were in the world, could do just that—give back. The programs had to reflect the diversity of the workforce and of their interests. "Not everyone wants to pull weeds in the park for hours—we want to offer opportunities so everyone can find something to match their individual passion," says Tammy Shea, Group VP, Corporate Communications and LifeWorks & Inclusion.

Play

The Discovery team developed three different but connected programs.

Discover Your Impact Day   Discovery launched Discover Your Impact Day in June 2010 in conjunction with its 25th anniversary, and celebrates the day annually to commemorate the anniversary. It's a day of global employee volunteerism where employees around the world give back to deserving organizations, underscoring the company's commitment to the people and places of the world where it operates. The days are organized locally, relying on a team of ambassadors who take responsibility for planning and executing local projects, understanding best what will resonate with local teams.

"Impact Day provides employees from different backgrounds, departments, levels and skill sets with the opportunity to cross paths with colleagues they might never meet otherwise and contribute to something bigger than themselves. It breaks down global barriers and allows our employees across the world to feel more connected to one another, since everyone is volunteering 'together' on one day, even though they might be thousands of miles apart," says Laurel Schepp, Manager, Corporate Relations.

Creating Change   Creating Change is Discovery's pro bono creative marathon initiative, which harnesses the aggregate creative muscle, strategic thinking and generous spirit of Discovery employees to help their charitable partners accomplish their business goals. Through Creating Change, groups of employees tackle projects for local and national nonprofits in a wide variety of areas, from design and video production to communications, marketing and building operation plans, as well as Human Resources and IT consultation.

Dollars for Doers   The Dollars for Doers program was introduced to celebrate Discovery's 30th anniversary, which is why the number 3 is used in the program design. Through Dollars for Doers, the company donates $3,000 to pre-vetted nonprofit organizations after an employee volunteers for 30 hours of personal-time community service, thus allowing employees to support causes their employees care most about.

"Discovery's array of volunteer programs offers employees many ways to bring the company's mission to life in the communities where they live and work. And it offers Discovery many ways to say thank you to the people and the planet that bring unforgettable stories to life every day," says Kristen Mainzer, VP of Corporate Engagement.

In Practice

- Find ways, no matter how big or small, to provide volunteering opportunities to your employees—it's something they'll value and engage with, and will make a profound difference.

Creating a Multi-layered Approach to Designing Values: *Southwest Airlines*

Situation

Southwest Airlines has a meaningful and yet simple purpose: to *"connect people to what's important in their lives through friendly, reliable, low-cost air travel."* This purpose is not just a slogan posted at headquarters, but a guidepost for employees on what overall success looks like for Southwest. To support this purpose, Southwest developed a set of values that provides employees with specific expectations on how they should interact with customers and each other.

Southwest is not unique in creating a set of expectations, but what sets the company apart is that it has created a multi-level approach, further defining expectations as employees progress upward through the organization. By setting specific expectations at leadership levels, it believes the company better supports employees, who in turn better support customers . . . thus providing a terrific customer experience. And it must be working—year after year, the airline has won multiple awards in customer satisfaction and as a top employer in the US.

Play

Southwest's multi-level approach includes these three levels:

1. **"Living the Southwest Way"—Expectations for All Employees**
   Includes *Warrior Spirit*, *Servant's Heart* and *Fun-LUVing Attitude*. Warrior Spirit is about working hard and striving to be the best. Servant's Heart is about respecting each other and following the Golden Rule. Fun-LUVing Attitude is about having fun and being a passionate team player.
2. **Expectations for All Leaders**
   Employees promoted into leadership are expected to demonstrate three additional expectations. *Develop People* is just what it says—focusing on knowing, serving and growing the people on your team. *Build Great Teams* is about building trust and cultivating an inclusive environment. *Thinking Strategically* requires leaders to see beyond today and plan into the future.
3. **Additional Expectations for All Senior Leaders**
   Leaders who step into senior leadership roles have three additional expectations. *Demonstrate Capacity* focuses leaders on delegation and prioritization. *Communicate Effectively* is important for casting a compelling vision and communicating openly and often. *Be Knowledgeable* requires leaders to be ever learning and self-aware.

Southwest Airlines takes leadership and its leadership values seriously. The team believes that strong leaders are the support network for employees who perform well and ultimately win customers. For this reason, they hire leaders by evaluating against these values; build training for leadership courses using them; and even use them to measure annual performance, with 75% of appraisals based on Living the Southwest Way and only 25% on achieving work objectives.

"Having values applicable to each level within Southwest helps us keep things simple, such as how we hire, develop and grow talent. Specific expectations for leaders lets them know that how they lead is just as important as the business results they are achieving. Leadership is critical to supporting employees, and we want leaders at all levels to take that seriously," says Bonnie Endicott,[10] Director, People.

In Practice

- Make sure your values work throughout the organization, adding new ones at different levels if you believe this will make a difference.
- Weave your values into your HR practices to ensure they are embedded into how employees behave and perform.

Changing Your Values to Help Drive Your Mission: *Interface Carpets*

Situation

Interface, a world leader in modular flooring, is a company led by a strong and meaningful mission, one that truly makes a difference. Named Mission Zero™, it's the company's promise to eliminate any negative impact the company has on the environment by 2020. According to Katy Owen, Chief Human Resources Officer, "We entered the sustainability world long before it had a name, at a time when there were no paths to follow. Through passion and innovation, we've designed our own solutions, layer by layer."

In 1994, Interface's founder and CEO Ray Anderson, an "avowed capitalist," challenged the company to adopt its zero footprint vision. His challenge was sparked by a personal epiphany, prompted by a customer's question, "What is Interface doing

---

[10]For a video interview with Bonnie, visit rg.co/bonnieendicott

for the environment?" By setting a bold vision, followed by creating a plan to achieve it and not wavering from it, Interface empowered its employees and demonstrated that optimism can lead to action and change. When Anderson died in 2011, though, the company "went into mourning," says Owen. "He was an inspirational leader, the heart and soul of the company. It was almost like we'd lost our voice."

Enter a new leadership team in 2015, and a decision to help the company find its voice with a new set of values. To start, the team went on what Owen describes as an "archeological dig," getting out their "brush" to carefully uncover the truths of what got the company to where it was, and determine what was necessary to help move forward. "As we were closing in on our 2020 mission, we needed to take the next step, creating loyalty and engagement to help us achieve this important goal," Owen says.

Play

In partnership with its 3,500 employees from around the world, Interface uncovered the "genuine truths" that evolved into its five new mission-led values. The partnership and collaboration with employees was critical, since the values needed to come from within, hearing directly from employees what made the company great and what would make them personally committed to the mission. Interface's new values are:

Design a better way	Be genuine and generous	Inspire others	Connect the whole	Embrace tomorrow today

Having new values, however, wasn't enough to ensure the mission would be achieved, so Owen and then-COO, now current CEO, Jay Gould went on a four-month road trip, conducting meetings to share the values and engage in two-way communication and activities to help employees truly understand them, translating them into aspirational actions and behaviors.

Feedback on the values has been phenomenal. Employees have commented that "it feels like us," which confirms that the dig and the design have been successful. At the same time, it's been an eye-opener for some tenured employees to get re-energized with renewed focus after realizing that their values-led behavior had been slipping in the lost voice of the company. This will help Interface get to 2020, and go beyond a zero footprint to create a climate fit for life.

In Practice

- Keep in mind that your values have a critical role to play in delivering against your mission. If they don't do this, *change them.*
- Make sure you embed your values so employees understand and relate to them.

5

Leadership

Chapter Objectives

In this chapter, we will:

- Explore how the role of leaders is changing rapidly and technology is giving employees power that they never had before.
- Look at the 10 key attributes exceptional leaders demonstrate.
- Examine the role of the high-engagement CEO.

Key Points

- The world is changing, technology is democratizing power and leaders have to serve their people more than ever before.
- Leaders used to be hired and fired by their bosses. Now, if they lose respect, they can be rejected by the people they lead.
- All of the highest-engagement companies have engagement championed at the CEO level.
- Many of the traits of the best rebel leaders are connected to building and maintaining trust.

Introduction

I'd love to write a whole book just about leadership, but this isn't it. So in this chapter, we focus exclusively on the key role of leaders in creating an organization and culture that staff want to engage with. It turns out there is a very strong overlap between that and what makes a great leader. At the end of the day, what more is there to leadership than **setting direction** and **creating an environment** where people can, and want, to do their best work?

The Role of Leaders is Changing

While leadership has always mattered in terms of your ability to get the best out of people, it now also affects how customers think of your business. The Edelman Trust Barometer found that employees who trust their leadership are significantly more likely to advocate for their company and its products and services.[1]

The voice of employees has never been more powerful, with social media, open communication and public reviews leaving nowhere for leaders to hide. Sites like Glassdoor allow employees, past and present, to leave anonymous reviews of a company and its leadership. Once in the margins, Glassdoor is now in the mainstream: 41 million people visit the site monthly, 80% of candidates read Glassdoor reviews before applying for a job and customers—and even external investors—are starting to look there, too.[2]

Leaders Need the Support of their People

More than ever, people are demanding visible, accountable and valuable leadership. We're moving from an era of command and control to a system of *"leadership by consent."*

---

[1]http://www.edelman.com/insights/intellectual-property/2016-edelman-trust-barometer/state-of-trust/employee-trust-divide/.

[2]Figures from Glassdoor and Reward Gateway's own research in the UK and the US.

Employers like Google are taking power away from team leaders—they don't allow them to rate their direct employees or hire independently, outside a hiring committee. Instead, to deliver on the complex jobs people have, where we need them to bring their creativity, ideas and judgment to work, employees are demanding that leaders add visible value. If leaders do not, people start to withdraw their consent to be led, the murmurings get louder, braver employees ask probing questions and the leader's personal authority starts to collapse.

Businesses perform better when honesty and candor are encouraged, and that means providing multiple avenues for employees to speak up. In these environments, the best leaders thrive and those lacking can fail. I've seen this first-hand in Reward Gateway, where a leader who did good work but didn't invest enough in communicating and connecting with people was repeatedly the subject of questions and comments posed through public and internal channels. Ultimately, this person left, unable to battle the weight of opinion that they just weren't showing good enough leadership.

The New World Leader

Leaders are recognizing that how they are perceived by their employees is as critical as how they are perceived by their bosses. Positional authority has been weakened; today, leaders have to genuinely care about their people because they now run the double risk of being fired by the boss or rejected by their own staff.

Our own study of 350 millennials produced a multidimensional picture of what people now want and expect from their leaders. We asked respondents to state and prioritize the leadership traits that they respected and valued. The results show that what people are looking for in a leader has changed dramatically in the last 20 years. Leaders are no longer expected to be perfect—"*Own their mistakes*" was third favorite. Instead, they are expected to be positive and human role models.

Ten things great leaders do

1 Own + live the company values

2 Communicate openly + early

3 Inspire people to reach higher

4 Own their mistakes

5 Recognise big wins, small wins + hard work

6 Trust people

7 Make the right decision not the popular decision

8 Add value to their teams, helping them to succeed

9 Have the courage to be naked and visible

10 Take care of people

Leaders are hired to deliver results, but increasingly, to be effective, their teams have to see the value that they add. The team has to be coached and developed, and wants to see their leader marshall the resources that they need. Without that, leaders quickly lose the confidence of their teams.

> *"I keep beating the drum—management is here to serve the workers. We have to get people at the bottom not to take any bullshit. We have to be in touch with all of them. We have to get the best from everyone."*
> —Satya Nadella, CEO at Microsoft

There are great leaders who understand and do all of this, and there are leaders who say they understand but actually just pay lip service to it. I've lost count of the number of companies that have a "them and us" aspect of their culture because the staff feel that leadership operate to a different set of rules. What message does it send when the leadership team has the parking spots closest to the office? When they have the nicest desks or the corner offices? What about when leaders receive more vacation days, better life insurance or medical coverage? When they come and go as they wish while the rest of the company works to "core-hours" or has to ask permission to be trusted with flexible working?

Fundamentally, if leaders want to build trust they need to eliminate all of the barriers that separate them from their people. This always applies to the CEO, but also extends further, across the leadership team and beyond, with larger companies having to provide visible divisional, regional and group leadership.

Many companies find visibility is not enough: Improving levels of access is also key, giving employees the opportunity to pose questions, raise issues and make suggestions directly with senior leaders. Technology is making this more possible. Open communication systems like Slack, Yammer and HipChat are, in some companies, making it the norm.

The High-Engagement CEO

The CEO's job is ultimately to deliver business results, to deliver the mission. The key way they do that is to create an environment where employees *are able* do their jobs well and a culture where they *want* to do their jobs well.

CEO Support is Critical

From all of the companies we met, those with the highest engagement all, without exception, had CEOs who were passionate about people and understood the power of engagement in the business.

It's just a fact. If you want to reach the heights of business performance that come from world-class employee engagement, it is not going to happen if your CEO does not champion it.

Your people invent, market, sell, build, deliver and support the products that your customers buy. When your customers buy those products, your company and its shareholders make money. Every hour your CEO spends on creating conditions that make engagement more likely is an hour invested in the productivity of the entire workforce.

CEO roles differ widely from organization to organization, depending on the company's growth stage and context. In public companies, there's an investor relations angle; in smaller companies, the CEO may still have operational responsibilities. Whatever the additional burdens the leader of the business has, they must own three key things personally from an employee engagement perspective.

1. **Own and be able to articulate the vision**

   The CEO must own and explain the company's strategic vision, its mission, its strategy and its reason for being. A clear statement of direction and destination is one of the greatest gifts a CEO can give to a business.[3]

   The CEO should articulate the mission with ambitious goals because the best people want to achieve great things—they want their lives to have meaning. They know that reaching the moon is not certain, but they absolutely want to have the best goal possible.

   "Make sure you can articulate the story and the vision really clearly and succinctly; you're going to need to repeat it a couple of hundred times each year."

   —Bill Collis, President at Foundry

---

[3]There is a useful military analogy called Commander's Intent. For info and full details, see **rg.co/commandersintent**.

2. **Be the architect of company culture**

   The CEO must own employee engagement and company culture because he or she is the only person with the cross-functional authority to lead and direct the actions that are needed.

   Writing words in a book or on the wall is not enough. Your culture is the result of the hundreds of actions you take each year under each of the 10 elements of the Bridge™. It will take courage and commitment to make choices that are actually in line with the culture you want, and that's why the CEO must own this personally.

3. **Deliver results**

   There is a two-way relationship between business results and employee engagement. With a disengaged workforce, you won't get the business results you could get. Similarly, if your business isn't successful, any success at employee engagement will be short-lived.

   Very simply, if the company doesn't have product–market fit and doesn't win in its niche, then the best people will move on and those left will become disengaged.

   Employee engagement can survive and even thrive for a short time in a *"batten down the hatches"* or *"we're at war against the world"* environment, but that can't last forever. Engagement needs good business results, as much as good business results depend on engagement.

Rebel CEOs we met use every tool at their disposal to cut through the hierarchy and bring themselves closer to their people. They treat their staff as the key stakeholder group, alongside customers, that powers their organizations' success. They use tools like Glassdoor to have direct conversations with staff; listening, understanding and, where necessary, explaining business decisions. Spencer Rascoff, CEO at Zillow, the property listing business, has responded personally to more than 70 employee reviews as a way to stay connected.

In Practice

Key Outcomes Rebels Strive for

Cultural Adaptability   Well-led companies have high levels of trust in leadership. This gives them the ability to adapt quickly and make changes that other businesses would struggle with.

With trust in leadership, workforces are more accepting and adaptable because they know their leadership cares about them, is telling the truth and is focused on the same mission as they are. This gives such companies a significant advantage.

Improved Results   The defining metric of employee engagement is not an employee engagement score, but business results. Fundamentally, rebel CEOs break through decades of HR dogma and create engaging cultures that power incredible business results.

> *"I try to create an environment where people feel safe, valued and important. It would kill me if we went to the premier of a film and someone from the team said they knew that a scene could have been better, but they hadn't said anything."*
>
> —JJ Abrams, Producer and Director

Key Rebel Behaviors

Rebel leaders show a real understanding of people. When examining their key behaviors, it is clear how much of what they do relates to the creation of trust. The trust they build increases information flow upward—their team is open and honest, knowing they will handle information with integrity. This greatly improves the decisions these leaders can make and the judgment that they develop.

1. **Put the mission first**
   Rebel leaders put the mission first wherever possible, prioritizing it over short-term profits or other goals. They're

prepared to make bold, long-term decisions to make the mission successful in the long term.

2. **Live the values every day**
Rebel leaders are role models for the company's values. They take every opportunity to communicate and apply the values, constantly showing how the values can guide and help decisions.

3. **Have and use great judgment**
Rebel leaders prioritize doing what is right over what is popular. They are accountable to their people and act as servants, but are prepared to be unpopular when necessary, striving to do what is right for the business, the customer and their people as a whole. They are open and honest early with their team and don't shield their team from bad news.

4. **Are human**
Rebel leaders bring their whole selves to work. They are humble, have the courage to be genuine and show vulnerability, and lead with compassion and kindness, showing their people that they truly care about them. Doing this gives the whole team permission to do the same.

5. **Act with integrity**
Rebel leaders develop honesty and candor, and practice total integrity. They strive for real honesty, not "*business honesty*." They tell the full story wherever possible and as early as possible. They give the whole truth, the back story, the why. This leads them to make better decisions, better calls, with sharper judgment, which builds trust.

> *"We need leaders who add value to the people and the organization they lead; who work for the benefit of others and not just for their own personal gain. Leaders who inspire and motivate, not intimidate and manipulate; who live with people to know their problems in order to solve them and who follow a moral compass that points in the right directions regardless of the trends."*
> —Mary Kay Ash, American businesswoman, and founder at Mary Kay Cosmetics

Making a Start

Get your CEO and Leadership Team on Board If your CEO needs convincing—if this is new to them—then don't worry; some do. Give them this book; in fact, give it to the whole leadership team if you have to. But more than this, make it personal to your leader and to your company. If they're all about profit, then show them specifically how engagement can affect and enhance profit. If they're all about client retention, make the numbers specific to turnover. Get help from **rg.co/rebelstats**.

My co-author Debra tells me that when she worked at a fashion retailer, she would always present engagement proposals in the context of jeans: how many more they would need to sell or how many would be left on the shelves, depending on engagement results.

Make Engagement Part of your Leadership Language
The second thing I'd say is to make engagement a part of your language. Put it on the agenda for your leadership meetings, make it a specific KPI, put it on the objectives for each and every leader at your company. Whatever you do, find ways for leaders to make it a priority and to act and feel accountable for the results.

THE PLAYS

Leading Millennials to find their Path:
VaynerMedia

Situation

In March 2016, VaynerMedia, a digital media agency, appointed Claude Silver[4] as its first Chief Heart Officer. As CEO Gary Vaynerchuk explained at the company's all-hands meeting, "We want to build the best human empire in the history of time." For

---

[4]For a video interview with Claude, visit rg.co/claudesilver

Silver, this meant, "Let's create an emotionally and physically safe place for people to bring their whole selves to work, so our employees can achieve both success and happiness."

With 80% of the workforce made up of millennials, the key to achieving this was to "help employees find meaning in what they're doing, and guide them in how to identify and remove their own roadblocks," says Silver. "Millennials are looking for any kind of magic tricks for how to get promoted and move up the ladder quickly, so if I can help them understand their strengths and play to those, they'll genuinely thrive, which is a win-win for them and VaynerMedia."

Play

Silver's approach has been to create one-to-one coaching sessions, which she calls "whiteboard sessions," with an aim to "help employees find their personal mission statement or guiding principle, key to unlocking growth on a person-to-person level." She asks a range of questions to help the answers unfold, with examples including "Why does your team feel you're valuable?," "What are you good at and love to do?," "What do you value the most?," and my favorite, "When you're standing in front of the mirror brushing your teeth, who are you?" It's a very visual process that includes whiteboarding responses to help map out and identify patterns and themes.

At the end of the session, employees leave with drafts of their personal mission statements/principles. Throughout the coming weeks, Silver sends them coaching questions and assignments, and they then return for another session to finalize their "sentences." "This approach has been extremely effective in helping employees take part in defining and 'being present' in their futures," says Silver.

This approach and these coaching sessions have contributed to low attrition rates at the company, which is no surprise, since it supports the needs of millennials to understand and be provided with real growth opportunities. They've also contributed to the achievement of one of Silver's key objectives set by her CEO: to touch as many employees as possible, having her energy rub off on them. This has certainly happened, with employees benefiting from Silver's blend of passion and compassion, turning employees into champions, as she explains—finding their path, their voice and their whole self.

In Practice

- Put in the effort to understand what will matter most to your employees, and then use all the skills in your "leadership basket" to support them.

A "Real" Consultative Approach: *St John Ambulance*

Situation

The leadership team at St John Ambulance (SJA), the UK's leading first-aid charity, decided to try out a new approach to making certain key decisions: to go to the charity's 2,500 employees *before* making key decisions. I'm not talking about sending out surveys or conducting employee focus groups, but doing what I'd call "real" consultation.

According to Steve Foster, Director of People & Organization, "I know it's incredibly obvious to do this, but many companies just don't. They're afraid of what employees may say, the extra time it may add to processes, or the concept of 'turkeys will never vote for Christmas' meaning will they make the right decision if it affects them personally? If you want to build true engagement, you have to give your employees a real voice in decision-making."

They've seen positive results based on this new approach, having used it for decisions relating to organizational design, pay & benefits. "The impact has been that decisions have been considerably better than had we not involved our employees. They surprised us with different perspectives and things we would have never thought of, even though, with hindsight, we should have thought of them," said Foster.

Play

The approach SJA used was rebellious in how and when it was done. The "how" was by holding functional and regional workshops, which on its own is not rebellious—however, they ran these events with defined objectives and parameters, but without a proposed solution. Instead of going in with a prescribed list and then asking employees to agree or disagree, they went in with objectives and a "clean sheet of paper." "We were upfront in what 'sandbox' they were playing in, but then gave them the freedom and opportunity to come up with their own ideas," says Foster.

The "when" was throughout the project, not just at the beginning, but as an iterative process, getting employee perspective at various important touch points.

This approach could make some leaders nervous, believing they should make decisions or have the most information/experience to do so. However, SJA found that by genuinely including employees in the process, they ended up with better decisions for the business and their workforce. An example was when they created admin hubs, with their thinking changing considerably based on the expert knowledge of front-line employees, resulting in a different approach to the design and location of hubs. They also found that employees gave their true opinions even if it put their own jobs at risk, so the assumption about "turkeys not voting for Christmas" turned out to be untrue.

In Practice

- Help leaders understand the positive impact that involving employees in "real" consultation can make in decision-making.
- Find ways to use the employee voice throughout the entire process, not just at the beginning.

Creating a Leadership Model that Drives Results: *Halfords*

Situation

Halfords, the UK leisure and car accessory retailer, has an ethos based on customer service that "drives every single person in the Halfords team—whether you're on the shop floor, under a bonnet [hood of a car], or going above and beyond to help your customer." According to Jonathan Crookall, Group HR Director, customer service begins and ends with the store manager. "A store is like a family unit: If you don't get engagement with the leader right, you can feel the difference as soon as you walk in."

But when Crookall joined the company, he felt there was a leadership challenge, one that had to be overcome to ensure the family unit—the store—ran like a proverbial well-oiled machine. He set out to develop a leadership model to drive engagement and results across its 460 UK stores.

Play

The leadership model Halfords designed includes what Crookall calls the "big four." They are: *clarity, praise, using strengths* and *having a genuine concern for others*. "If leaders get these right, they'll have engaged colleagues, superior customer service and strong business results," says Crookall.

These aren't just words handed out to leaders; they've incorporated the model into how they run the business. "We talk about the big four all the time, reinforcing them from day-to-day and from week-to-week," says Crookall. An example is in how they were launched—bringing together all leaders for a three-day event to ensure a deep understanding of what the model was and how it should be used.

Another example is the "leadership index," which is a score coming out of its employee engagement survey. The index has an important role to play for the leader, since it sheds light on how their employees believe they are as a leader, and what they need to do to improve. It's used for performance planning, learning and development, and even as an element of the leader's bonus.

The model has helped Halfords improve employee engagement, customer service *and* profits. Over the past five years, engagement has increased by 15 points, customer satisfaction has moved by more than 10 points and total sales have increased by over 25%. In addition, it's helped Halfords move from the 18th to the 13th spot in the UK's *Sunday Times* "30 Best Big Companies to Work For."

Finally, "Focusing on great leadership is really paying off, not just for our employees, but for our customers and shareholders, too," says Crookall.

In Practice

- Be clear about who you want your leaders to be, and develop your support and measurement programs around this.
- Be relentless in reinforcing and measuring your leadership behaviors—recruiting, developing and rewarding against them.

6

Management

Chapter Objectives

In this chapter, we will:

- Start thinking about the management policies, rules and procedures that affect staff on an ongoing basis.
- Understand the importance of having managers aligned with the company's values and mission.
- Discuss the myth of the permanent job.

Key Points

- Management policy and practice must be in step with your values and what leadership say, or you will have an inauthentic culture.
- Treating our staff as adversaries, which is how many employee handbooks and policy documents start out, is a key factor in damaging trust.
- Perhaps the biggest lie we have in management practice is the myth that jobs are permanent—not dealing with this undermines management relationships.
- Managers are powerful and it is critical that they be on board with employee engagement.

Introduction

Leadership and Management are distinct elements on the Bridge™ but we show them on the same level to make the point that they are closely connected, maybe even intertwined. To some extent, leadership is what you *say* your organization will do, but management is what it actually *does*.

In all but the smallest organizations, the most critical decisions will be taken by your managers. They will decide who gets hired; who gets fired; who gets promoted; who gets a raise; how people are managed, coached and developed. It is those actions—detailed and described by HR policies and contracts, and put into practice by your managers—that have a real ability to support or damage engagement. And, for the majority of companies, they are damaging engagement.

Policy and Practice is Rarely Aligned with Values

Far too often, companies make great statements at a corporate level about what an amazing culture they want or have, and then they tolerate or create procedures and practices that directly contradict those statements. You can't operate an authentic culture with a value of "trust" or "integrity" if your expense or benefit policies are based around the assumption that every employee is a potential fraudster.

I'm afraid that HR and legal departments have caused so much damage here—they've been so focused on protecting what they perceived to be the company's best interests that they have become the expert at the one-sided agreement. I realize this will sting for some readers and I share the pain—we've struggled to meet the standard here, too.

The problem with one-sided agreements is that while employees often sign them without vocal complaint, they have a huge hidden cost. Employees see the "us and them" relationship encoded into the actual fabric of the company, and the cost is the trust and therefore potential engagement we have with our workforce. **If we want our staff to be engaged and on our side, fighting our battles and winning for the customer, we have to start with the premise that we're not adversaries, but we're actually on the same team.**

The standard employee handbook is a prime example of this—I've never seen an example of a document with such a misleading title. Any employee who thinks it could be useful to help them navigate their company and make a success of their role and career is in for a shock. Like so many of our management policies and procedures it was never written with the intention of inspiring, motivating or engaging the people it was written about. Many were never written to be read at all!

I fell afoul of this myself at Reward Gateway when, in 2013, I stumbled upon our US employment contract. We have a company value called Be Human and we preach trusting your staff and doing the right thing as an employer, but our US operation was tiny at the time and we'd bought an employment contract off the shelf. Not tailored to our values, it was so harsh—at every opportunity, it skewed the game completely to us as an employer, fighting battles that had no value for us, reserving for the company privilege that we did not need and would never use. It felt nothing like us and made us look inauthentic.

Our contract said	But our culture and values said
You can't leave us and go work for a competitor.	Our value *Be Human* says everyone is a real person with their own personal life and career to juggle. We can't offer anyone a guaranteed job for life, so how does this fit? And what are we really so scared off? This makes us look petty.

(continued)

If we end your job in the first six months, we'll give you one week's severance pay (nothing at all in the US).	How can someone live on that? How would they pay their rent or buy food for their kids? We know most people don't have savings. This doesn't fit our Be Human value—if we screwed up recruitment, we should cover two months' severance pay.
You qualify for benefits after a three-month probationary period.	Why? We enter our recruitment team for awards! Are we so uncertain of their abilities that we send out job offers to people randomly? How does that make a new starter feel—like a half-person for three months?
We can read your e-mail and documents at any time and without notice.	That's not right—the world has changed and we have work–life integration, not separation. Someone's personal stuff is their own, regardless of whether they use our laptop or not. Surely we should do this only in an official investigation, sanctioned at a high level, and notify the person at the time?

When I asked the recruitment team how people felt signing it, they told me it often raised issues because it felt so out-of-context with the candidate's recruitment journey up to that point.

I remember feeling ashamed that we'd asked anyone to sign it, and went and apologized to every person we'd hired in the US. I re-wrote that contract personally, removing every single one-sided protection for the company before tearing up all the old contracts and signing new ones with all of our US team.

Are We All Interims Now?

The heart of management malpractice might actually be the *myth of the permanent job*. We all know that companies can't afford to offer lifetime employment now, but even if they could, who would want it?

Imagine: You apply for a job because you think it's a great fit for your skills, interests and abilities—you're excited by it and you want to put your all into it. But once you've chosen it, that's it; it's the only job you're going to have because you've signed a lifetime employment agreement. In 18 months' time, when the needs of this role have changed or we've found a different way of doing it, you're going to stay here at the company because you signed a lifetime employment agreement. Who would actually want that?

The Truth is There is No Such Thing as a Permanent Job

Maybe that's a good thing—we're too skilled, too educated, too deserving of a great place to work that we should ever trust a single employer to be all we will ever need.

We want permanent jobs because they give an illusion of job security—but that's all it is: An illusion. If we faced up to this, we could chart a new path, owning career development and choices better and ending the differentiation in terms and benefits between staff we call interim and staff we call permanent.

You should do a job for as long as you love it, as long as the job loves you and as long as the customer needs it to be done. When that time ends, there might be another great job in the same company or there might not. But your job is too important to your long-term happiness to be doing one that you don't love—so never settle.

The problem is that all of our language and process is caught up in a fantasy world that doesn't exist any more—anyone who leaves us is "disloyal" and we've failed to "retain" them. When it's the company's choice it's assumed that the individual let us down, did something terrible or was defective in some way. But is the truth not often just that someone did a great job and the job that needs doing next is a different one?

The person who can get your product team from 10 people to 80 might not be the person who can develop it from 80 to 200. It's a mistake and fails both sides when you keep people in jobs because of what great work they have done for you in the past. Surely the only reason to keep people in jobs is because of what they can do for the mission in the future.

We Assess for Person–Job Fit at Recruitment, But Then Rarely Again

Isn't this more honestly an ongoing process for both sides? Our performance reviews and even pay reviews all look backward at "what did this person do," but shouldn't we all be looking forward? "What does the company need to do next? Is this person the best person we can have doing it?"

I get questioned about this all the time. "Oh, Glenn, I hear so-and-so has left, what happened? What did they do wrong? I thought you liked them. Did they let you down?" I often answer, "They were amazing, but their job is done now—the person who would get us from here through our next phase needs different skills and ability." This is an approach often done only in desperate times, but surely it should be routine. How can we move to a world where people are able to do their very best work, in companies that they love, in jobs that make them feel alive and energized, if they or half the team around them is there primarily because they did good work in the past?

The Myth of a "Family-Doesn't-Fire" Culture

In *Leaders Eat Last*, Simon Sinek argues that "being a leader is like being a parent" and makes the case that the ultimate role of a leader is to provide safety to their people and that, from safety, trust will grow and results will follow. He advocates a *"no-fire policy,"* saying you'd never fire a member of your family, so you should do everything you can to avoid firing a member of your team.

This, I feel, misunderstands what makes great cultures. A no-fire policy means your teams will be filled with people who aren't right, who aren't able to do the job that needs to be done, which will damage team and company performance. Just think through how that feels to the rest of the team.

Great cultures are not about perks and foosball tables, and they are not about an easy ride. **Great cultures are made by the achievement of great things by teams of great people, working based on a compelling mission in an environment where you can do great work**. Being surrounded by people who are there out of a misplaced sense of family loyalty destroys that and prevents those people from being in a job that they love.

> *"The idea of the permanent job is one of our cruelest lies—there are no permanent jobs. We do people a terrible disservice letting them think things will last forever. The biggest epiphany I had in my career was the day I decided I didn't want to try to keep people forever anymore; instead, I wanted to make Netflix a great place to be from."*
>
> —Patty McCord,
> Former Chief Talent Officer at Netflix and author of Powerful

We need more honest management practices that accept that we're all interim now and that we all deserve great jobs that we can excel at. If we had that, then maybe we could plan and navigate career development within and outside the company without the emotion of disloyalty and fear that hampers those conversations now.

Managers Have Real Power

Ultimately, it is your managers and the policies and procedures with which you run the business that have power to make or break the culture that leadership wants. Despite that, we rarely train managers in how to manage according to the company's values. This is why many culture change projects fail: Leadership charts a new path, but then fails to get management on board and doesn't get their hands dirty by changing the hundreds of processes, forms and mechanisms that actually make the organization work.

Managing your people with authenticity often requires rewriting the rules of how you treat your people and retraining or removing managers who don't want to live by those new rules. There are four common reasons why managers resist:

1. Management *doesn't understand* what leadership is saying, so *can't* follow through;
2. Management *doesn't believe* that what leadership is saying will work, so *doesn't* follow through;
3. Management *feels threatened* by what leadership is saying, so *undermines* everything; and
4. Management *isn't resourced* to deliver on leadership promises.

It is key to get your line managers on board and ensure they are able, willing and sufficiently resourced to manage people in the way you want. Managers have a huge amount of power—Gallup's data shows that 50% of employees leave because of their manager and 70% of the variation in engagement scores is related to managers and management practice.[1]

---

[1] 2015 Gallup survey.

Management Really Matters

Leadership can inspire you to a cause, connect you to a strategy and make you deeply want the organization to succeed, but it's management that your people will connect with each and every day.

Bad managers can ruin lives—people often recover when they finally escape, but the real damage is done in the interim. Get good at identifying bad managers and removing them quickly. Failing to do this will lose you the respect of your staff, who always feel the pain of bad managers first.

In Practice

Key Outcomes Rebels Strive For

High Levels of Trust from Authenticity   Companies that deliver daily on their purpose, mission and values through highly aligned management practices create cultures of extreme trust. This facilitates better two-way communication, especially speaking up from the front line, because people feel the company can be trusted to act on its promises.

Excellent Reputation as an Employer   Rebel companies develop outstanding reputations as great places for people to *be from*. They have clarity and courage to talk openly about jobs not being for life. They work hard to make employment a real win-win for employer and employee, creating workplaces that are effective at development so their alumni become highly employable.

Focus on Customer   When management practice is aligned to values and mission, everyone can focus on the customer, because there is nothing in the way. In inauthentic cultures where management practice jars, the organization becomes political and people waste energy on maintaining their status and keeping their jobs.

Key Rebel Behaviors

Rebels work hard to create great alignment through the company—from leadership through all levels of management. Key things we see include the following.

1. **Write HR and finance policy for the many, not the few**
   Rebels accept that most people are good and trustworthy, and they develop HR policy and practice that is respectful of their people and honors their good intentions. They deal with people who go outside this rule quickly and efficiently, removing them from the team without hesitation.
2. **Align HR practice with Mission, Purpose & Values**
   Rebels review HR and management policy and procedure ruthlessly to make it live up to the company values and cultural statements that leadership make. This shows that the organization is serious about, and committed to, following through on its culture.
3. **Have adult equal relationships with employees**
   Rebels accept the new reality that both employers and employees have choices and they chart a more equal relationship, acknowledging this and making ethical promises on work and career.[2]
4. **Ignore established HR best practices**
   Rebels are unafraid to be different and say goodbye to established "best practice" if it doesn't fit their goals. One way to do this

[2]See LinkedIn founder Reid Hoffman's book *The Alliance: Managing Talent in the Networked Age.*

is to ditch the annual performance review—12% of the *Fortune 1000*, including GE, Deloitte Gap Inc and Accenture, have abandoned the traditional performance review, recognizing that the process looks backward rather than forward and is primarily concerned with grading people, rather than helping them achieve their best.

5. **Love their lawyers but manage them carefully**
   Rebels form great relationships with their legal teams to make sure they comply with local laws and protect the company against real threats. They also use great measures and constantly weigh up—how often will something happen, when it happens, how much will it cost and the method of protection—to assess how something will sound and feel to other staff and whether it's worthwhile.

Making a Start

Get the Employee Handbook Out, Make People Proud of It Most companies have an employee handbook and, for many of us, it's a pretty awful book that talks only about disciplinary action and how you can get fired. While there will always be legal requirements you need to follow, depending on your country, a great place to start is to review this handbook. Challenge everything in it against your values. You can find ours here **rg.co/ employeehandbook**.

Ask Employees to Review Your Policies, Practices and Staff Contracts Asking a group of real employees for their honest feedback can be a real eye-opener. I was amazed at how much legal and HR jargon we put out that staff just don't understand. Working really hard on this language helped us create a more equal relationship with our people. Asking staff to sign things that even the manager can't really understand when they try to read it isn't a good start. I found that the person in our company who was most afraid of contracts was a real help in helping us write understandable versions.

Make a Bold Announcement   Share parts of this chapter with your team and make a bold announcement to your people that you want to bring management practice more in line with company values and leadership statements. Set up an anonymous feedback channel and ask people for examples of when management practice has not, or does not, meet company values. Whenever I do this, I'm amazed at the volume of examples that come, and we've been working on this for years.

THE PLAYS

Paying Staff to Leave ... Really: *Zappos*

Situation

Like many companies, Zappos, the online shoe and clothing retailer, believes it's important that employees truly embrace their company culture and values. But how many companies do you know that are so committed, they have a program where new hires are given a choice to stay with the company or take a sizable payout (one month's salary) and leave the company?

Are they mad? Why would a company throw money at people to leave? Zappos doesn't see it this way, believing it provides new hires an amount of money that will allow them to make the right decision, rather than stay in a culture that doesn't fit them just because they need the money. "Culture fit has to be a two-way street, so we want to make sure new team members don't feel that they are 'stuck' in a place where they won't really be growing. We understand that it's not for everyone and want to give them the option of being honest about the fit from their own perspective," says Jon Wolske, Insights Culture Evangelist.

Play

Only 2% of new hires take the money and leave Zappos, which is down to what they do *before* the new hire is given this choice. Beginning with the application process, culture and values are displayed front and center, with candidates having to go through pages talking (and singing) about them before they can even get to the page where jobs are posted. Next, instead of cover letters, applicants are encouraged to submit videos to show who they are, helping the company understand whether they are the right fit. Finally, the interview process, from initial screening to team-based interviews, centers around culture and values-based discussions, getting to know the candidate, and in turn letting the candidate get to know Zappos.

You'd think the "culture fit" process would be complete once the robust selection processes ends. However, they see this as the first leg of a rather long trek, with a month-long orientation process completing the cultural immersion. It "welcomes new hires into the Zappos culture and helps them to see how serious we are about our culture, which helps them get fired up about what they will get to be an active part of," says Wolske.

This novel approach has worked for Zappos, with one month's salary of "walking money" representing the final part of the process used to protect the Zappos culture.

In Practice

- Find ways to build your culture and values into recruitment processes, letting you and potential employees see the "real" thing.
- Create induction processes that are robust enough for new hires to see and feel what the company is really like, and consider being brave enough to do something about it if it doesn't work out. Better to rip the Band-Aid off sooner rather than later, right?

Ditching Performance Ratings and Annual Reviews: *Gap Inc.*

Situation

Gap Inc., the fashion retailer, had a traditional performance review process, but it simply was not delivering results—not for the business and not for employees. "It was complex, time-consuming and expensive. At our company's headquarters alone, it was estimated that people were spending 130,000 hours a year and significant payroll on the process." To add to this, managers and employees disliked the process—as one employee complained, "I think it's a waste of time, causes unnecessary stress, and is really an old way of thinking in this modern day and age," says Rob Ollander-Krane,[3] Director of Talent Planning and Performance.

All of this, combined with a growing consensus among HR and performance thought leaders that traditional performance management had had its day, led Gap to decide to radically overhaul its approach. The new philosophy and process was rolled out to headquarters' employees worldwide, and to one of their five brands in 2016, bringing it to store employees. It's been such a success story that the Harvard Business School uses it as a case study for its MBA program, and it won Gap Inc.'s prestigious Founders Award for Innovation—the first for an HR project.

Play

The new performance management process is called "GPS", and stands for "Grow. Perform. Succeed."—an analogy for what Gap wants its managers to do. "A GPS in your car lets you set your destination, and if you make a wrong turn as you're driving, it recalculates in real time and gets you back on the right path. We wanted managers to be like a real GPS—course-correcting

---

[3]For a video interview with Rob, visit rg.co/robatgap

employee performance throughout the year," says Ollander-Krane. Coincidentally, GPS is also the company's stock name, so the name of the internal measure of performance now matches the external measure of performance.

The five components are:

1. **Performance standards** replace the rating scale by giving a broad overview of employee behaviors expected. "It embodies every aspect of our new approach—having a growth mindset; delivering and learning from feedback; and just having regular, open and honest conversations. It puts the focus as much on the 'how' you have achieved your goals as on the 'what' you have done," says Ollander-Krane.

2. **Goals** focus on outcomes rather than tasks, with a maximum of eight to ensure employees focus on a smaller number of important objectives. "Driving performance is not about ticking off all the things you have on your 'to do' list; it's about thinking about how the world will be different if you achieve them all," says Ollander-Krane.

3. **Touch points** replace the single annual review meeting with 12 informal discussions. Taking place anywhere and at any time, they focus on three questions: What went well? Where did you get stuck? What would you do differently next time?

4. **Rewards** have been revolutionized. With no ratings or forced distribution curves, managers have been forced to rethink how they allocate merit and bonus payments. "It's a much simpler exercise, and more similar to the way we expect our managers to manage our products. If a product does well, you reinvest in it, and the concept here is the same—you give more money to the person who is delivering the best results," says Ollander-Krane.

5. **Learning** includes several modules developed to provide help and support with the new process, from feedback conversations to how to allocate bonuses.

The GPS process has delivered phenomenal results, positively affecting HR metrics; saving HR, managers and employees time; and helping to improve employee performance. They are definitely onto something here, showing you can drive performance and engage employees without ratings and reviews.

In Practice

- Look at how and when performance conversations are happening at your company. If they aren't working, then change to make them truly drive performance.
- Look at your performance ratings: Do they drive and reward performance or are they holding your business and employees back?

Creating a SMARTA Goal-Setting Process: *Xero*

Situation

Xero, which makes accounting software for small businesses, is all about connections: connecting clients with the right numbers and connecting the workforce with the company's strategy and vision. This was easy to do when the company started out but, as the workforce grew, it got harder to maintain this essential connection.

As Anne Allen,[4] Director of People Experience, explains, "We believe it's important that our employees are all pulling in the same direction, with our key operating priorities demonstrably living and breathing outside of the boardroom." For Allen, this meant looking again at the challenge of goal setting, beyond the mere "ticking of a box" (checking off a list). To achieve this, she set about persuading managers and leaders to apply motivation

---

[4]For a video interview with Anne, visit rg.co/anneallen

techniques and psychology to what is normally considered a pure business exercise.

The result is a new goal-setting process that helps drive a deeper connection with the individual and the organization—essential if people are going to have the opportunity to do the best work of their lives. It's still early days, but Allen says, "There's an energy and buzz as conversations and discussions occur and true alignment takes shape."

Play

Xero's new goal-setting process is called "SMARTA", adding to the traditional SMART goal-setting process. The new "A" stands for Alignment, and includes two key messages.

1. The first emphasizes alignment with the company's strategy, with managers helping employees set goals to fit in and drive key operating priorities. This is important so employees are "pulling in the same direction," says Allen, but also so employees can understand how they contribute to the overall success of the company. With so many employees motivated by having a sense of purpose, this is critical for employee engagement.

2. The second part, and the part which Allen believes is the most exciting since it adds a new dimension to goal setting, is an emphasis on personal alignment. It encourages managers and employees to discuss and uncover personal motivators and drivers, and explore the ways work might help individuals realize their purpose and achieve their dreams. The sense of individuality and purpose are absolutely key parts of the discussion so each employee can "bring his or her whole self to work." Allen believes this type of alignment discussion drives a much-deeper connection with the business and is

well worth exploring. Time invested by the manager in under-standing an individual's true aspirations provides rich returns in terms of trust and connection—critical elements for both an employee and organization to thrive.

Xero has found this change in the process and how to think about goal setting is helping create a greater sense of meaning and purpose within teams. Employees engaged in these types of conversations have a clear opportunity to understand the con-nection between what the company is trying to achieve and their role in that achievement. Great for bottom-line results and great for inspiring a fantastic employee contribution.

In Practice

- Make sure your goal-setting process focuses on both connection and alignment, with managers helping employees create goals that get everyone moving in the same direction.
- Don't be afraid of adapting processes such as goal setting if you believe they will make a difference to your employees and your company.

Recruiting to Build Long-Term Relationships: *Vitsoe*

Situation

Vitsoe is a British furniture manufacturer. It has a single-minded determination to design furniture that lasts for generations, support-ing it with the very best customer service, being in it for the long run. The same can be seen with the company's recruitment approach and process, similarly driving the result of hiring employees to enter into long-term relationships with the company. Does this take more time and involve more resources? Yes. Is it worthwhile? Absolutely. For just as Vitsoe doesn't sell disposable furniture, the company doesn't hire "disposable" employees.

Play

There are three very important parts to Vitsoe's comprehensive recruitment process. The first part is a telephone screen, which is done intentionally over the phone so "we aren't distracted by appearances," says CEO Mark Adams.[5] The call takes from 20 to 40 minutes, just enough time to form an opinion about whether the person should be taken to the next stage. The second part involves bringing the person in for a face-to-face interview, and again, assessing the fit.

The final step, and what makes the process unique, is that candidates are brought in for a full trial day, showing the commitment to the process. The candidate spends half the day where the furniture is made, and the other half of the day in the shop where the furniture is sold. The aim is to see the "real person" in a variety of environments and situations, both formal and informal, whether in the locations, traveling to and from, or grabbing a bite to eat. At the end of the day, everyone who has had contact with the candidate is brought together to discuss and debate their observations. If anyone has any doubts whatsoever, the decision is made not to offer the candidate a job.

The entire process is built around assessing candidates based on character first and skills second, and "not getting distracted by the great résumé," says Adams. "We want to put candidates in situations where we can see the 'real person' and not the 'interview person,' making sure that, as the expression goes, what we see is what we get." The result is a truly long-term relationship, with the average length of service standing at 15 years.

---

[5] For a video interview with Mark, visit rg.co/markadams

In Practice

- Build steps into recruitment processes to ensure you're hiring employees who fit your organization for both the short and long term.
- Make it a priority to build ways into your interview process to meet the "real" and not the "interview" person.

Putting Your People First: *Talon Outdoor*

Situation

Talon Outdoor, a media agency, has a people-first philosophy. The organization prides itself on hiring smart, enthusiastic and driven individuals, and then taking it that one step further and treating them like adults. This has certainly worked for the agency, proven by accolades such as ranking first in their second year of entry in the UK's *Sunday Times* "100 Best Small Companies to Work For" after being in the top 10 the previous year.

As part of the company's health and wellbeing strategy, it was important to find ways to support employees and improve work–life balance/integration. As Mapara Fernandez, Head of People, says, "In a world where we're constantly bombarded with information and reachable through every means possible, it's important more than ever to be able to take time out to switch off."

Play

The result was a bold new approach to e-mail called "Seven to Seven": Guidelines that encourage employees not to send non-urgent e-mails between 7 p.m. and 7 a.m., all seven days of the week. "The aim of the initiative is to get employees into the habit of not monitoring e-mail once they've left the office, so they can focus on those important and grounding non-work-related areas of their lives, be it their families, hobbies or just unwinding," says Fernandez. They also wanted to ensure that employees were aware of the impact of e-mails on themselves and their quality of life, as well as their colleagues, and then let them make the best decision.

To support these new guidelines, they did three things. The first was helping employees think through the impact of e-mails sent outside windows—that is, how it feels when you receive an e-mail at 8 p.m., and how it affects your home life and your state of mind.

Second, the company provided practical tips on how employees could continue to work effectively, such as by delaying the delivery of e-mails.

Finally, the approach was shared with clients through a press release. "Clients respected what we were doing, seeing that we genuinely cared about the wellbeing of our staff. They also saw that the initiative didn't undermine the quality of work and high level of service we provide as a business," says Fernandez. This new process has resulted in the company improving its Best Companies Wellbeing score, ranking third-highest in this category in 2016.

In Practice

- Consider the impact of work practices on your employees, and find ways to make even the smallest of changes.

"Always On" Approach to Employee Feedback: *Dunelm*

Situation

Dunelm, a home furnishing chain in the UK, is a company that's been built around strong relationships—with its customers, its suppliers and its more than 9,000 employees. One way the company has maintained a relationship with its workforce is through an annual employee opinion survey. However, they began to question it, asking themselves, "If we survey our customers constantly, why are we surveying our employees only annually?" and "Does this really align with our culture of fast and honest feedback?"

The team set out to create an employee survey that mirrored its customer survey—one that was "always asking and accessible at all times." It's early days, since the survey was rolled out only a year ago, but the feedback received from employees so far has already helped make a positive difference to the business, and with lines of communication between managers and employees.

Play

Dunelm's "always on" employee survey is based on a net promoter score (NPS) and asks two simple questions: "Would you recommend Dunelm as a good place to work?" and "Tell us what is going well, is not going well and could be improved." The first question returns a net promoter score which gauges the engagement of employees. The second question returns free-form responses, which allows the company to analyze employee trends and sentiments based on key words or phrases that are used in these responses.

"We've been surprised by the balance of feedback received, with employees sharing the good, the bad and the indifferent, it's been a real mixed bag," says Wayne Hall,[6] Reward Manager. On average, the company receives 50 comments a week, with the majority of employees answering all three parts of the second question, covering an average of six topics. These rich and frequent data have become a useful management tool, with managers being able to see and act on feedback immediately, helping them make better decisions for their stores day in and day out. Examples have been concerns over the vacation request and rota processes which, when raised, could be acted on swiftly and effectively. "We've been able to nip things in the bud quickly through this survey, not having to wait until the end of the year when it may be too late or things may have already moved on," says Hall.

The "always on" survey has become an integral part of Dunelm's three-part "Keep Listening and Looking" program for collecting employee feedback. The other two parts are the annual employee engagement survey, which provides annual benchmark data, and pulse surveys, which are used for targeted and specific feedback. Together, these surveys ensure that employees have a variety of tools to be heard, and for managers to act.

In Practice

- Ask yourself if an annual survey provides enough feedback from your workforce. If it doesn't, find ways to collect more timely feedback.
- Have your managers responsible and accountable for acting on employee feedback. HR can own the system and processes, but managers own the actions.

---

[6]For a video interview with Wayne, visit rg.co/waynehall

7

Job Design

Chapter Objectives

In this chapter, we will:

- Discuss how we got to a place where too many people have jobs that provide no pleasure, satisfaction or pride.
- Present a model for thinking about jobs based on how demanding they are and how much control the person has.
- Explain the key ways we can create high-engagement jobs.

Key Points

- Bad job design can sabotage any chance of employee engagement.
- Some jobs are just too easy to be engaging because they lack autonomy and freedom.
- The best-designed jobs have recognition and learning built into them from the start.
- Job design problems can actually be the root cause of issues with recognition.

Introduction

I'm going to start by being blunt: We are universally terrible at job design.

Most jobs aren't actually designed at all—we're lucky if they are a list of loosely connected tasks and we rarely, if ever, think about how the person doing them will feel. As a result, we end up with boring, repetitive jobs; frustrating jobs; and jobs where the person can't tell if they've had a good day or a bad one.

To make matters worse, we then document these positions with job descriptions—some of the most awful documents to come out of HR, which I often think have a primary aim of being waved at someone as we fire them, saying, "See, you didn't do any of these things." And then, as if this weren't enough, we convert the descriptions into job advertisements that paper over the cracks and make the key responsibilities even less intelligible or understandable.

The tragedy here is that job design is an area where HR could really lead, if only the HR specialty Organizational Development got more attention. There's less written about job design than any other part of engagement—interestingly, many people we spoke to hadn't even considered it an engagement driver, and a few hadn't even heard of it.

To put things right, we have to start asking some simple questions:

- How will someone feel when doing this job?
- Can I imagine a person who will enjoy it and find it fulfilling?
- Where can I see this job developing?
- How does this role connect to our mission?

If we can't answer these questions positively, it's a clear marker that we may need to rethink the role. **If we want engagement in our organizations, we need to first eliminate the *disengaging* job.**

The attributes of a good job are not complex. People need to deploy and develop skills, believe they are producing something meaningful, have enough challenge and demand to be stimulated over the long term, and have enough freedom and autonomy not to feel part of a machine. Most leadership and HR jobs will tick many of those boxes, which might be why we've become so bad at this area: **Maybe all the people with power have decent job designs and can't empathize with the people who don't.**

It Wasn't Always Like This

Barry Schwartz is a psychologist and professor of social theory and social action at Swarthmore College, Pennsylvania. In his book *Why We Work*, he asks the question, "Is Job Design, and in particular the factory production system, the root of employee disengagement?"[1] He shares the idea that the factory system swapped pride and purpose for efficiency and increased production.

Most of us have been accustomed to the factory system of production for all of our working lives. Many jobs are organized for efficiency, not personal fulfillment; the roles were created to manage or be part of a process, rather than allow someone to feel satisfaction by achieving a goal.

But it wasn't always like this. The factory system was created by Adam Smith, often considered the first theorist of capitalism. Smith believed that men would seek the easiest life possible, and must be made to work by associating money with the completion of tasks. He saw efficiencies by breaking a job into small components and allocating them separately, inventing the modern production line. He knew this would result in the elimination of any sense of job satisfaction, but since he believed the average man didn't enjoy working anyway, the only thing of any importance was the payoff or reward that work produced.

---

[1]TED talk version at **rg.co/barryschwartz**

> ## People Become Efficient Parts of a Production Machine
>
> The factory method resulted in huge improvements in efficiency and production volume—great for society when we were predominantly a manufacturing economy, but the cost was the reduction of work, for many, from something meaningful with pride, satisfaction and contentment to something that was meaningless, boring and repetitive; something you would only do for money.

In the early days of Reward Gateway, we had jobs like this in parts of our back office. There was an acceptance that some roles just had no joy in them and would best suit someone who was unambitious and just wanted to turn up, do their tasks and leave. I still feel a twinge of shame now in thinking back to those days— at the thought that we'd just accept that whole sections of our own workforce should be resigned to jobs with no inherent fulfillment.

Job Design Has a Wide and Often-Overlooked Impact

The issue of job design is so poorly understood it is missed by some of our best thinkers. In his TED Talk "Why good leaders make you feel safe" and the book *Leaders Eat Last*, management consultant Simon Sinek discusses a gate agent at an airport who was yelling at a man attempting to board an aircraft before his number was called. When he asked the agent why she treated the man poorly, her response was, "Sir, if I don't follow the rules, I could get in trouble or lose my job." His conclusion is that a lack of safety and trust in her leaders is why she behaved badly to the passenger.

I think, though, there is an alternative explanation. The issue with the gate agent's behavior wasn't what she was doing; it was how she was doing it. She could have gently explained to the customer that it wasn't his turn, rather than shouting and making him feel small; that would still be following the rules. But she didn't; she was mean and aggressive, and the reason isn't a lack of safety. The reason is that she was stressed, frustrated and angry with her role.

Being a gate agent at an airport is a tough job with high demands and low control.[2] Agents drive the jet way, open the door, check in crew, board hundreds of passengers in increasingly complex sequences and deal with reactions to over-booking, all while using archaic systems. But they have almost no control: The rules are there to be followed, it's a safety- and security-critical job, and there is no autonomy. Even the freedom to pick which passenger is deserving of an upgrade if there is a spare seat in business class has been long given up to automation, based on frequent flyer status. As far as job design goes, being a gate agent sucks.

Designing High-Engagement Jobs

The good news is that we *do* know how to design great jobs. We know what makes a job fulfilling or frustrating. And it is possible to apply the key principles to make even the most entry-level job more complete and satisfying.

A starting point is to look at a job in two ways: (1) How demanding is the job for the person? and (2) How much control does the person have over how a goal is achieved, where it is achieved and when the work is done?

Jobs that are not demanding or challenging enough lead to boredom, frustration and even depression. Jobs that are very

---

[2]See http://www.airfarewatchdog.com/blog/6254416/what-it-like-being-an-airline-gate-agent-civilian-day-behind-the-podium/#

demanding but give the person no control lead to burnout. Jobs that are demanding, challenging and exciting, combined with high degrees of autonomy and control, are the magic ones, the "sweet spot"—the jobs that people love and that drive high engagement.

Designing high-engagement jobs

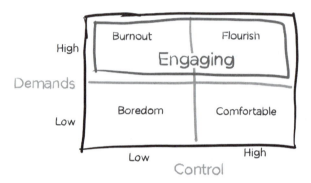

When we think of roles in our organizations or teams that need some TLC, three of the questions we can ask ourselves are:

1. **How can I build more freedom into this role?**
   How can I give this person some power to make decisions, even small ones, based on their judgment? Can I improve flexibility in how, when or where the job is done?

2. **What output or result could employees actually own themselves?**
   How can I change the role or team so people own a completely visible product, outcome or end-to-end process? This can be the difference between going home on a Friday and saying, *"That was awful; we had too much to do"* and *"What an amazing week; we achieved so much."*

3. **How will this role develop?**
   Development is really a function of job design rather than training—to be able to develop, you actually need room to

grow, space and freedom built into the role. That means asking "How can this role grow as the person's skills develop?" That's different from asking what role the individual could get next.

"All too often, when someone starts a job, we slap a rule book on their desk, with a strong warning to never step out of bounds. We almost never help them define a playground."
—Lindsay McGregor, co-author of Primed to Perform

Watch for Job Design Issues Presenting as Recognition Problems

When you hear people say they don't feel recognized, consider job design before assuming a new recognition program is needed. Some time ago, our engineers said this—the answer turned out to be to change part of their role. They were used to rotating between products to stay fresh, but this meant there was no ownership and also no one in the business knew whom to thank when a client sent praise for a product. The answer, which had many benefits, was to allocate engineers to products long term so they could develop ownership, we could introduce accountability and people knew whom to thank.

In Practice

In many ways, job design goes to the heart of a culture. Designing great jobs means creating a culture of trust over approval, of freedom over process. It means accepting the missteps and mistakes that will happen and resisting the urge to knee-jerk into creating a process or restriction of autonomy whenever something goes wrong.

Key Outcomes Rebels Strive For

Jobs with Autonomy and Accountability   Highly engaged people thrive with freedom and accountability. They are self-motivated, figure out what is best for themselves and the organization, and can be left on their own and trusted to perform with minimal supervision and minimal processes.

Culture where People are Responsible for Outputs Rather than Tasks   When roles are well-designed, people feel they are responsible for results that connect to the mission, they see the product of what they do as the goal and they understand how it connects to the organization's success. This contrasts with a more traditional view, based on tasks and actions.

Acceptance of Flexibility and Change   In the best companies, you never hear people say, "*That's not my job.*" People understand that their organizations are constantly learning and changing, and that their roles will be evolving and growing along with the organization. Adding "*other duties as assigned*" to the end of a job description just doesn't cut it anymore!

Key Rebel Behaviors

Rebels design roles and teams with several common characteristics.

1. **Freedom to fail and develop**
   Rebels design roles that have enough freedom for people to fail, because this provides freedom to develop. They realize that most things that go wrong in business can be fixed or reversed at moderate cost, and that this cost is less than the hidden cost of preventing growth, development and innovation by too much process.
2. **Accountability and visibility**
   Rebels understand that accountability and visibility are fundamental to great jobs that people love. They develop roles that

have clear results that can be seen, and they work to expose those results so people can see and share their achievements.

3. **Jobs designed around mission**

   Rebels understand that the only way they can achieve their company's mission is by making it part of each and every employee's role. They design jobs with this single ultimate objective in mind, and this creates focus and gives meaning to all roles.

4. **Focused, nimble teams**

   Rebels think about the individual and the team when designing jobs. They think about how teams will work together, operate together and succeed together. At Amazon, Jeff Bezos has the two-pizza rule: No team should be larger than two pizzas can feed, which limits teams to six or seven people. This keeps communication manageable. With a team of six, there are 15 links between everyone—15 possible conversations—but with a team of 12, the number of links shoots to 66.[3]

5. **Jobs that are meant to evolve**

   Rebels create looser role definitions that focus on responsibilities and outcomes, rather than tasks and consistency. This allows them to stay fluid as process and technology improve and allows people to grow, develop and move forward in their roles.

Making a Start

Overhaul the Job Description   The first step in moving toward these goals is to focus on the job description—and overhaul it. Whether you produce job descriptions, job ads or both, eliminate anything that can't be written on the back of a small pad or explained at a dinner party. Say what the person is responsible for, not what they should do, and strip it right back so the accountability is really clear.

---

[3]Math courtesy of Janet Choi, http://blog.idonethis.com/two-pizza-team/.

We know that the receptionist has to answer the phone, open the door and perhaps put out the trash. But surely what they're really responsible for is creating and executing a world-class visitor experience that leaves guests thinking they've just been to the most incredible place.

When you have a job description right, the job-holder should be proud to summarize it from memory, not scramble to find where it might be filed.

When it comes to job ads, focus sharply on the real attributes and skills that will make someone shine in this role. Don't be afraid to be radical. This was how we stripped back the ad for an internal communications assistant at Reward Gateway:

Want Ad : Internal Comms Assistant

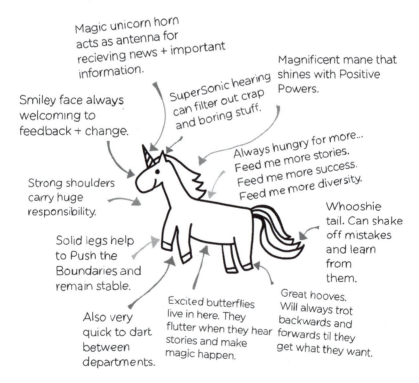

Magic unicorn horn acts as antenna for recieving news + important information.

Magnificent mane that shines with Positive Powers.

Smiley face always welcoming to feedback + change.

SuperSonic hearing can filter out crap and boring stuff.

Always hungry for more... Feed me more stories. Feed me more success. Feed me more diversity.

Strong shoulders carry huge responsibility.

Whooshie tail. Can shake off mistakes and learn from them.

Solid legs help to Push the Boundaries and remain stable.

Also very quick to dart between departments.

Excited butterflies live in here. They flutter when they hear stories and make magic happen.

Great hooves. Will always trot backwards and forwards til they get what they want.

Increase Autonomy and Accountability Overcome your fear of what people will do by making them accountable for clear, visible results. Then give them the freedom to innovate, iterate and pioneer new ways of doing better. Unless you are in a heavily regulated industry or a safety-critical one, you should look to increase freedom every single day. You'll probably be battling decades of work that reduced freedom, but this will make a real difference.

Create Meaningful Job Titles Change any titles that don't clearly show accountability, so the rest of the business knows exactly who does what and whom to thank. "Software Engineer—Reporting Database" is a much better title than "Mid-level Engineer" because it helps everyone in the company know what that person actually does, and makes sure that the person wakes up every day with a reminder of what they are responsible and accountable for.

THE PLAYS

Building Innovation Into Jobs and Working Practices: *Atlassian*

Situation

Atlassian, which makes software that helps engineers collaborate, believes that when talented individuals team up and work together, they make great things happen. It should be no surprise that they follow the "make your people the geniuses" model, for as Dominic Price,[4] Head of R&D & Work Futurist, says, "We don't believe in the lone genius. We believe that innovation exists in everyone and needs to be part of the entire company's culture—not concentrated in a single person, or tucked away in a dedicated room. It is our job as leaders to create the right environment for them to express that innovation."

---

[4]For a video interview with Dominic, visit rg.co/dominicprice

That's just what Atlassian's done: created an environment for innovation by designing a mindset and space to innovate into jobs and work practices. Since then, it's seen amazing results—for the company, with many new product ideas coming from these innovation practices, and for its employees, by having more rewarding and engaging jobs, proven by Atlassian winning "Great Places to Work" awards at many company locations over many years.

Play

Atlassian has created three "rituals" that form its culture of innovation. The first is to *innovate every day*, as evident in its value of "be the change you seek." "Our values are behaviors that we live every day, not just posters on walls. This gives us incremental innovation, and keeps us aware of our environment and variables in it," says Price.

The second is structured innovation, otherwise known as "20% time", where teams plan one day a week or one week in every five to seven to focus on innovation. It's done by department or function, working on something related to their team or work, but not from their backlog of work or jobs. It's a chance to try a pet project that relates to someone's area of work, driving continual improvement as a ritual: Prevention instead of a cure; fire-proofing instead of fire-fighting.

The third, and what Price calls the most disruptive, is called "ShipIt". Every quarter, for 24 hours, employees work to innovate whatever inspires them the most. "It's like 20% time on steroids or speed dating for hacking," says Price. Employees get ideas from all corners of the globe, from all disciplines and on a variety of problems and opportunities, with prizes being a small trophy and bragging rights. "The first ShipIt was 14 people in one living room. A few ShipIts ago, we had over 400 teams in eight locations participating," says Price.

Anything can be a ShipIt. The company has seen everything from practical to inspiring, simple to insane, technical to non-technical. One example is of a team suggesting replacing hot, energy-inefficient light bulbs with better bulbs. Another example is of a team hacking together a simpler portal to report JIRA (Atlassian's tracking software) issues, which was the start of their JIRA service desk.

"When you truly build an environment and adopt practices that support a culture of innovation, your teams start to take on the impossible. Your business starts to feel like a laboratory that celebrates experiments, generates new ideas, seeks constant feedback and nimbly evolves to delight your customers and squash your competitors," says Price.

In Practice

- Find ways to build innovation into your jobs and then give employees time and autonomy to innovate.
- You don't have to be in engineering for the ShipIt approach to work; it will work in any company and in any function, so give it a go.

Making Transformational Change Through Job Design: *Crawford & Company*

Situation

Crawford & Company, the world's largest insurance claims management company, was in a challenging situation—it was losing market share, losing clients, and both staff retention and engagement were low. Recognizing this, the UK CEO asked the

HR team to conduct an organizational transformation project, using an approach called "systems thinking." According to Pauline Holroyd,[5] previously EVP Human Resources at Crawford & Company and now Managing Partner at Quo-change Consulting Ltd., "Systems thinking looks at and changes the customer journey based on what really matters to the customer. It focuses on having the right expertise at the right place at the right time." For a company like Crawford, whose workforce is dedicated to helping people, this was the perfect approach, as it put the focus where it needed to be to achieve its mission and purpose.

The outcome of the project has been the creation of jobs designed to align with the new customer journey, achieving a wide range of positive results. These include reduced operating costs by eliminating activity that adds no value to the customer, decreased settlement times, as well as increased employee and customer satisfaction.

Play

The "systems thinking" method Holroyd and team used throughout the project includes four key steps, the 4Ds:

1. **Diagnose.** Work with key leaders to understand the current situation, looking at potential opportunities and agreeing the way forward.
2. **Design.** Analyze cases and data, both historical and current, along with observations to thoroughly understand performance in service and financial terms. Develop and test versions of the new work design, looking for step-change improvements.
3. **Deploy.** Roll out a new operating model to include workflows, tasks and roles.

---

[5]For a video interview with Pauline, visit rg.co/paulineholroyd

4. **Develop.** Implement ways to sustain the new model and embed change, which includes building measures that help leaders understand how their service is performing so they know where to action to fix problems and drive continuous improvements.

The results achieved by using this method across the business were absolutely staggering. From a company perspective, customer satisfaction increased by 70% due to settlement times reducing by 40%, and settlement resolutions increasing by 25%. From an employee perspective, job satisfaction increased as work was now more interesting and employees were having more positive interactions with customers. This led to reduced absences, decreased attrition and employee engagement increasing from 40% to 80%. These results show the transformation achieved through this strategic approach to job design.

In Practice

- Make sure your jobs are designed to align with your company's mission and purpose, driving performance in the right way to achieve this.
- Ask yourself, are your jobs focusing time and energy in the right areas? If not, review them, borrowing from the 4D method described in this play.

Welcome to Flatland: *Valve Corporation*

Situation

Imagine working with super-smart, super-talented colleagues in a freewheeling, innovative environment: no bosses, no middle management, no bureaucracy; just highly motivated peers coming together to make cool stuff. Sound interesting? Well, it should, since this is exactly how Valve Corporation, the video game developer, describes the company and its workforce. Why do they do this? As it says on the website, "When you give smart, talented people the freedom to create without fear of failure, amazing things happen."

Play

I can explain how Valve delivered against company objectives in one word: Flatland. This is how it's defined and described in the employee handbook:

> *Welcome to Flatland: no one tells you what to do*
> Hierarchy is great for maintaining predictability and repeatability. It simplifies planning and makes it easier to control a large group of people from the top down, which is why military organizations rely on it so heavily. But when you're an entertainment company that's spent the last decade going out of its way to recruit the most intelligent, innovative, talented people on Earth, telling them to sit at a desk and do what they're told obliterates 99% of their value. We want innovators, and that means maintaining an environment where they'll flourish. That's why Valve is flat. It's our shorthand way of saying that we don't have any management, and nobody "reports to" anybody else. We do have a founder/president, but even he isn't your manager. This company is yours to steer—toward opportunities and away from risks. You have the power to greenlight projects. You have the power to ship products. A flat structure removes every organizational barrier.

The company is so committed to this concept of no organizational barriers that desks have wheels, as symbolic reminders that employees can/should move themselves to be more valuable. As the handbook says, "There is no organizational structure keeping you from being in close proximity to the people who you'd help or be helped by most."

It may be a bit radical to have a completely flat structure and desks on wheels, but it's worked for them, delivering results year after year that have helped the business innovate and succeed.

In Practice

- Consider how a multi-layered organization job design could be holding back your employees from being the best they can be. Ask yourself whether all layers are necessary or if some are just getting in the way.

- Consider what kind of "wheels" you can design into your jobs. What can you do to make jobs more flexible and nimble, moving people to the work that has to get done?

Creating Autonomy and Accountability through Job Design: *Drift*

Situation

When David Cancel,[6] former Chief Product Officer at HubSpot and now CEO of Drift, rebuilt his product team at HubSpot, he wanted to see "if we could get beyond slogans and mantras to structure it in a way that intrinsically placed the customer ahead of everything else."

"Every company in the world will tell you they are customer-driven. They'll believe in the principle. They'll have framed posters on the wall about it: 'Solve for the Customer.' But none of that means anything unless you actually make the structural decisions to ensure it. I made a few decisions, in form, process and culture, that were designed to safeguard the team against misdirection and ensure that customers remained central," says Cancel.

---

[6]For a video interview with David, visit rg.co/davidcancel

Using this new model and approach, he grew his team from about 50 people to around 200 by the time he left to start his new company, Drift, which writes software that helps sales teams. It was so successful that it set internal records for employee engagement, employee retention, customer happiness and team performance, and is shared in Cancel's book *Hypergrowth*.

Play

The new model involves two fundamental changes from traditional models and approaches. The first involves *decreasing* the size of teams. As Cancel said, "One of the highest impact decisions we made at HubSpot was to constrain both the size of the teams working on a product and the scope of work they undertook. Small teams mean fewer distractions and a singular shared focus on the customer problem at hand."

Teams are made up of three members. Why three? "Because I made it up. It's a starting point. We can refine from there," says Cancel. The company tested teams of all sizes, but in the end came back to a three-person team as the most manageable for the tech lead. It gave them enough time to get their work done and meant that everyone on a team could sit together. As a result, most teams did away with traditional meetings and daily standups, since they were already working together and communicating on an ongoing basis.

The second change was *increasing* the amount of ownership, freedom and autonomy that teams have. This meant letting the teams decide what they were working on, when they were working on it, etc. "It allowed the people closest to the problem to come up with the solutions and test those solutions with the actual customer. After all, those are the people who are spending more time with the customer than anyone else in the company—more than the executive team, more than the CEO. They have the right perspective in solving this problem and measuring whether they solved the problem or not," says Cancel.

These changes not only improved the overall effectiveness of the teams and the company as a whole, but provided greater job satisfaction and overall engagement of team members.

In Practice

- Find ways to build autonomy and accountability into job design. It's a win for the company and for employees.

8

Learning

Chapter Objectives

In this chapter, we will:

- Discuss what we mean by a learning culture.
- Show how learning requirements and tools have changed, and the importance of organizations adapting to them.

Key Points

- Technology has fundamentally changed learning by making huge amounts of free content available.
- Learning is a personal investment—it should be owned by individuals, giving them freedom to learn in their own time, at their speed and on their terms.
- For learning to happen, companies need first to have a learning culture, inspiring and driving learning.
- Job design and culture are key—without freedom and responsibility, there is no learning.

Introduction

You can hire the best people, design the best jobs and have the most engaged workforce, but if you don't get learning right, your organization is destined to underachieve. But we all know that, don't we? When we talk about providing training or learning opportunities to our staff, no one really disagrees—we're all in vehement agreement that it's a good thing. But then training is the first thing that gets cut, last in the line for budget because we know we can always do it next year.

> *"People at McDonald's get trained for their positions, but people with far more complicated jobs don't. It makes no sense. Would you want to stand on the line of the untrained person at McDonald's? Would you want to use the software written by the engineer who was never told how the rest of the code worked? A lot of companies think their employees are so smart that they require no training. That's silly."*
> —Ben Horowitz, Partner at Andreessen-Horowitz and author of The Hard Thing About Hard Things

At Reward Gateway, we never invested heavily in what you'd call formal training—a very modest budget existed and only as recently as 2015 did we even have a single member of staff dedicated to training. But despite this, we created a learning culture. An analysis of 108 anonymous reviews of Reward Gateway on Glassdoor between January 2012 and February 2017 showed that 62 of them mentioned *"professional development"* as a positive—way ahead of *"employee benefits,"* which got the next most mentions at 32, and *"leadership"* at 31.

How have we ended up with at least some semblance of a learning culture with what we feel internally involves very limited resources or effort? The answer is in technology and culture. Technology, the internet in particular, has disrupted learning hugely. When I started my career 25 years ago, we learned by being sent on expensive residential courses—we even did these to learn a new software package or technical skill.

Now we have YouTube, TED Talks, conference presentations and keynotes filmed and available on the internet just hours after being recorded; ebooks, real books, book summaries, blogs—vast swathes of information, coaching and training available online at our fingertips. We've realized that for a lot of the professional development we want to provide, the task for our L&D team is now less content creation and more content curation—helping our staff pick through the mass of content out there to find the best, most relevant support. And through the search engine, we have the world's reference library at our fingertips—the effect that has on our ability to learn as we go is incredible.

> *"When someone is stuck and doesn't attempt to find the answer themselves, when they don't think about the problem enough to form a good question they are delegating their thinking. And when you delegate thinking, it appears that you view other people as your assistant, or that you are lazy. Both of these options come with social cost."*
> —Sam Dunn, Founder & CEO at Robin

The Learning Culture

A learning culture is one of the greatest gifts you can give your organization because it inspires the very people already on staff to develop and be able to do more. Three key components of a learning culture include:

- Freedom and autonomy—jobs designed with room for people to step outside their comfort zone, learn and try new approaches.
- Ambition—key to learning is wanting to keep doing better and look for the next stepping stone; without that, there is just inertia and a drift to safety, which means no growth, no development.
- Acceptance of failure—we can't grow and develop if we're afraid to put a foot wrong. Babies learn to walk while falling over; if your culture doesn't embrace that, staff won't develop.

Overall at Reward Gateway, I think the biggest things we did that helped people grow and develop was to give everyone a lot of responsibility and then be ambitious for results. We were good at celebrating the wins, but always used them as a platform to reach for the next, higher goal. We very much had what we now call a *growth-mindset* baked into the culture from the start.

Employees are encouraged to learn; are recognized for learning; look at failures as opportunities; and regularly share links to TED talks, blogs on various topics or talk to other companies to understand best practices. There is a constant mindset of *constructive challenge*, helping each other and sharing information we find, along with an expectation that there is always something new to learn or try. This experimentation mindset extends to technology, too—the bar for us in trying out a new tool or technology is very low; we're always trying new things. It's too low for some people, who see the abandoned tools as failures, but for most, it's all part of the iteration and experimentation that you have when you embrace a learning and developing way of working.

A Learning Culture is Key

An organization's learning program will never work if it doesn't first have a learning culture. Employees value and engage with a culture of learning—one that nurtures, encourages and supports constant and continual learning.

Shift the Power

Too many times, I've seen organizations push, force or threaten employees to learn, where learning is something you do "to" employees. "You must attend this class, you must take this test"; the list goes on and on. This doesn't really work, because, at the end of the day, only your employees can decide if they're going to learn. They have to "show up" and "want" to learn.

Companies need to accept this and make a critical shift in the power, moving it from the company owning learning to employees owning it and having the power; changing it from a push to a pull.

We relaunched our in-house Reward Gateway University in 2017. During the planning stage, we started with a traditional matrix of courses and job roles, marking off which courses were mandatory or optional and available for different types of roles. Then we realized this was wrong—learning is a very personal activity, requiring personal commitment and investment in terms of time and attention. With the exception of security and privacy courses, which are mandatory for all of our staff, we shouldn't be forcing learning upon anyone. If our culture is about trust and treating people as responsible adults, we should be providing all the training and courses we're asked for and then letting people decide as individuals which ones are useful to them, depending on the stage they are at, the problems and issues they face at work, and the ambition or interests they have for themselves.

Companies Can't Own Learning; Only People Can

People have to own their learning and development—no one will ever care about their development as much as that individual. Organizations can help by making resources available; but employees, themselves, must own their learning journeys.

Lose the Swim Lanes

In the past, jobs were designed in swim lanes—nice and neat; you do your job and I do mine. But based on changes in how we do business and how we do our jobs, as mentioned in the previous chapter, the lane separators have been widened or removed, with our workforce and their jobs swimming in a more integrated way, often in one big swimming pool. Processes are less rigid, people are sharing more, thanks to team and cloud technology, and companies are asking employees at all levels to contribute to the business and the bottom line.

Management guru Peter Drucker came up with the term "knowledge worker" in 1959, in his book *The Landmarks of Tomorrow*, at a time when businesses were shifting from manual jobs to those that required education and experience to create and share knowledge. But in the evolving world where innovation is a key differentiator between businesses, is knowledge enough? Instead, should we be developing what Jacob Morgan, author of *The Future of Work*, calls "learning workers"? These are employees who have not only the knowledge required to do their jobs, but a learning mindset and attitude to learn as they go, adapt and apply their learning to new situations and issues.

Our learning programs have to adapt to support this new kind of worker and this new kind of swimmer. They need to have access to learning they can pick up and use as they change lanes. Learning that will help them develop attitudes and skills in collaboration, problem resolution and innovation.

In Practice

Learning is a critical part of the Engagement Bridge™. I've rarely seen good people leave an organization when they're learning and constantly developing. It just doesn't happen. When people have the right amount of challenge and learning in their roles, they're just not open to other opportunities in the same way; they're engaged in what they're doing, engrossed in what they are learning. It is stagnation in learning that starts the seeds of disengagement.

Outcomes of Success

The best companies know the positive impact learning can have on their organization, striving for the following.

Greater Productivity and Innovation   Learning programs that help employees at all levels develop the right skills, behaviors and mindsets to lead to higher performance and innovation.

Higher Retention   Employees stick around because they feel the company cares about their development, investing time and money in programs to support them with this. Seven in 10 employees surveyed said that learning opportunities directly influence their decision to stay with a company.

Culture of Learning   Learning is a visible part of the organization and its culture, with people at all levels embracing and taking ownership for it. Employees take charge of their learning and their career development, with managers partnering to support and manage their learning outcomes.

Key Rebel Behaviors

1. **Know their workforce**
   Rebels know their workforces well enough to understand how, when and what they need to learn. They know how to create a high-quality learning program that's easy to use and access, no matter how employees like to learn or where they are. They also know their employees' diverse learning styles, and design learning to support each of them.

2. **Understand learning as a business driver**

   Rebels understand that learning is more than just delivering an engaging and fun experience. It's about focusing on learning goals and developing the workforce for the future, having the skills and behaviors that will provide what the business needs to succeed and to retain their key talent.

3. **Create a bit of "magic"**

   Rebels understand the need to capture the hearts and minds of the workforce so they'll make the decision to begin or continue on their learning journey. Besides having relevant content, they do this by creating their own "magic" in learning programs. They know that this is unique to them, and not something they can take off the shelves.

4. **Leverage their talent**

   Rebels understand that they have a wealth of talent within their organizations, and leverage it to provide additional depth and breadth of learning offerings and experiences to their workforce. Whether it's creating or delivering learning, the workforce helps them keep up with the pace of change and learning requirements.

5. **Constantly refresh**

   Rebels understand the need to constantly update and refresh their learning offerings, and aren't afraid to make the tough choices and remove programs. They constantly ask for employee feedback and review the latest and greatest offerings to ensure they have what will best meet the needs of the business and the workforce.

Making a Start

Develop Your Strategy You need to go back to basics and ask yourself "why." Why are you providing learning programs to your workforce and what change are you hoping to deliver through them to the business? This will help you set the direction to follow, making sure that all you do aligns with your needs.

Assess Your Current Offerings   Based on your strategy, go back and assess your current offerings, asking yourself: Will my programs deliver against them? Will they meet the needs of my diverse workforce and their diverse learning styles? Will they take my company to the next level or keep us where we are now?

Map Out Learning Journeys   Create a visual of your company's learning journeys, showing what is offered to employees as they learn and progress in your organization. Use this for two purposes—first to identify gaps, and second to communicate with your workforce, engaging them with the programs and their development at your organization.

THE PLAYS

Learning Based on Einstein's Theories: *Stonegate Pub Company*

Situation

The UK-based Stonegate Pub Company was faced with the challenge of creating a learning program and career path to support and drive a newly merged business with a combined workforce of 13,500 in 700 locations. No easy task. But for a company that believes in promoting talent from within, and creating a workforce that delivers best-in-class customer service, this was critical to their success.

They decided the best way to achieve this was to create an engaging and unique program, one based on no other than Albert

Einstein and his theories of continuous learning. According to Lee Woolley,[1] Head of Learning and Development, "We're in the people business and we know our staff are brilliant at interacting with customers and delivering great service. What we wanted to achieve with Albert was to bring a fun approach to the important business of learning and development. We're not a boring company, so we didn't want a boring program."

In the four years since the program launched, they've made an additional \$4.1 million in profit from those attending management courses, have increased internal promotions to 75% and have halved turnover.

Play

The star of Stonegate's award-winning program is Albert, the infamous theoretical physicist. He's everywhere, and not just in name, but having an active role in helping employees along their learning journey. On the online learning portal, named Elsa after one of Einstein's wives, Albert narrates the content, runs competitions, interacts through social media and even has his own cartoon avatar. This clever use of theming and strong branding based on Albert creates engagement with the program, as well as an ongoing connection with employees.

The learning journey begins with "Albert's Law", an online program completed by employees 24 hours before they begin their first shifts, and continues for an additional six weeks. It's packaged in short e-learning modules, and gives employees control of the learning process. The journey continues with programs to take employees from team leader through to general manager, providing a combination of online and classroom-based learning aimed at stretching participants to be the best leaders they can be.

Stonegate (and Albert) have truly created a continuous learning approach to support the company's employees and their business. As the real-life Albert Einstein said, "Life is like a

---

[1]For a video interview with Lee, visit rg.co/leewooley

bicycle; to keep your balance you must keep moving," which is exactly what Stonegate is doing with its exciting and innovative learning program.

In Practice

- Add some fun to your learning programs—you'll have a better chance of engaging your employees with them over and over again.
- Make use of theming and branding to create something employees can easily recognize and engage with.

Deliver On-demand Learning to Gig Workers: *Zeel*

Situation

Zeel, a company with more than 10,000 massage therapists delivering on-demand massages throughout the US, had a number of interesting challenges when it came to providing learning programs to employees in its network.

First, the information had to be delivered to a workforce composed of on-demand, independent workers. Second, and possibly an even bigger challenge, was that most employees worked not just with Zeel, but for other organizations. Someone would, for example, work as a massage therapist at a doctor's office during the day and then, later in the evening, work as a therapist with Zeel. From a learning perspective, this meant finding ways to communicate effectively with employees using just-in-time learning (i.e. learning when they needed it) and mobile tools. Since Zeel therapists can start appointments as early as 8 a.m. and as late as 10:30 p.m., 365 days a year, in more than 70 cities, any solution had to be mobile, portable and on-demand.

Play

Zeel's solution was to place reminders directly in the Zeel Massage Therapist app, which all employees use to access appointments. This resource allows therapists to perform Zeel massages "their way and in their own time," says Zeel founder and CEO Samer Hamadeh. Checklists and reminders are built into the app, giving therapists easy and constant access to tools to help them. The suite of learning tools also includes short educational videos, followed by quizzes to further engage and educate employees on the protocols and behaviors Zeel customers expect.

"Learning is a constant process for us, since our business and customer service expectations are constantly changing," says Hamadeh. He cited an example of receiving customer feedback about a therapist who tracked in mud from their shoes. To prevent similar situations, the company quickly responded within hours by adding a programmed reminder to the app for therapists to be on the alert for such issues. For Zeel, its customer feedback—both praise and suggestions for improvement—is invaluable in helping therapists evaluate their performance.

The on-demand learning tools have helped Zeel's on-demand gig workers feel more confident in their day-to-day practice and the challenges of their business.

Practice

- Create bite-sized training videos, with or without quizzes, to give your employees constant, evolving and engaging learning tools.
- Don't shy away from delivering learning tools designed specifically for gig workers—don't ignore their unique needs and challenges.

Creating Development Plans to Help a Young Workforce: *KFC Australia*

Situation

KFC Australia had what Rob Phipps,[2] Chief People Officer, would describe as traditional individual development plans (IDPs) for the fast food organization's 34,000 team members. That's fine for some organizations, but for a company that's committed to making a difference in the Australian community, with one out of 700 Australians working there at some point in their careers, they felt they needed to do more—to help their young workforce, with an average age of 17, understand and map out their life goals, and to align with the KFC people promise of "be your best self," "make a difference" and "have fun."

Working with the Career Industry Council of Australia, KFC created a new online program called "#myplan", which helps team members create personal career and development plans, and recognize career opportunities both within and outside KFC. According to Phipps, "We didn't want to replace the job of a career counselor at school because our managers aren't trained to do that. We wanted to start a conversation and then get team members to go home and talk to their parents or career counselors to go further."

Play

The #myplan program includes two modules, one for managers and one for team members. The manager module helps managers feel comfortable with the process, providing coaching and mentoring tips and practical information about steps and actions to be taken. The 20-minute team member module asks questions about what they want to be and do, and what goals they want to achieve. The result is an action plan providing a framework for self-reflection, self-evaluation and setting life goals. It can be

---

[2]For a video interview with Rob, visit rg.co/robphipps

used in discussions internally with managers, as well as externally with career counselors and parents.

The program has only been in place for a year, but 4,000 team members have already gone through it. Phipps says the company is already seeing positive results and even individual success stories, such as one team member who was thinking of going into a career in nutrition and, by flagging this through the program, received training and support to achieve this by working in the KFC food innovation team.

#myplan is a great example of a company giving back to its employees. As Phipps says, "It's filling a gap by offering a program to help team members set a direction and achieve their goals. Whether it's deciding they want to become a teacher or a nurse, saving for a holiday or a new car, or deciding they want to lose weight, #myplan helps them with this journey."

In Practice

- Don't be afraid to think outside the box to provide learning opportunities for your workforce, taking that extra step to truly support them.

Using Learning Academies to Drive Results: *MVF*

Situation

MVF, which operates sales acceleration technology, realized it needed this same level of acceleration when it came to inducting new employees. How could the company speed up learning through the induction process, making employees productive as quickly as possible?

The answer was with learning academies, something that Titus Sharpe,[3] President and founder, heard about from talking

---

[3]For a video interview with Titus, visit rg.co/titus

to the former CEO of Qlik tech, one of the fastest-growth software companies in the world. He was shown a graph illustrating the profound difference in sales their academy had made, so he set off to develop his own version of academies for MVF.

The results have been just as profound, with 2.6 times higher sales for those attending the academy. In addition, it's contributed to increased collaboration between academy attendees, and increased retention of staff.

Play

MVF's sales academy was developed by asking one simple question: "What makes our best salespeople great?" Using the best practices the team uncovered, a six-step process became the foundation of the sales academy. The program lasts for three months, with the first week focusing on understanding the company and the remaining weeks getting into the details behind each of the six steps.

Learning comprises 60% of the academy, with the other 40% involving practical work, creating the right balance between learning and doing. To continue with the concept of balance, attendees must pass written exams, make presentations and participate in practical selling activities. "Our three-month long sales academy has had a profound influence on MVF's growth trajectory. The impact has been so large, we are rolling the learning academy concept out across the business, starting with marketing and SEO," says Sharpe.

In Practice

- Look for opportunities to make your induction programs accelerate the learning and productivity of your new starters.
- Don't isolate your learning to one department or team. If it works, spread it around to other parts of the business.

Put Gaming into Your Learning Program: *GAME*

Situation

The gaming industry has changed massively over the years, with a greater number of games on a wider range of devices. It's great for consumers, but for companies like GAME, the computer game retailer, this creates the challenge of constantly training front-line employees, making sure they have the most up-to-date information on the latest and greatest games.

A few years ago, store managers were responsible for sharing this information with employees. However, due to this faster pace, it was taking a huge amount of their time. Craig Mills,[4] Learning Manager, was a Store Manager then, and put forward a proposal to the business to develop an e-learning system, one that would share this critical information and free up managers to, well, manage.

The result is GAME's innovative e-learning system that aligns with the organization's business and culture, while using the great techniques and motivational tools featured in the games employees sell. According to Mills, "We wanted to create a place that people wanted to go, making it a special reward for working at GAME." Has it worked? On launch day, employees were on the system until 3 a.m. so they could earn the top spot on the leaderboard, and currently there are around 14,000 logins each month, with employees going into the system about once a week. I think you'd agree it's working.

Play

GAME's e-learning system has all the features of a winning computer game, with learning modules designed to get employees involved, wanting to come back over and over again. Like a game, it's designed to be interactive, so instead of a normal quiz at the

---

[4] For a video interview with Craig, visit rg.co/craigmills

end of a module, employees can engage with content in a variety of ways to test their knowledge and keep the experience fresh. It also makes use of the competitive nature of gaming, with employees earning points for completing modules, helping them "level up" to the next level of training, earning a spot on the leaderboard. These encourage employees not only to complete the training, but do well enough to score the highest number of points—a winning combination.

There's also an important social aspect to the system that is common in gaming: creating a learning community. Employees post messages and videos, join chats, and tag people in different stores as knowledge is shared real-time.

The system has created a positive and engaging learning experience for employees, one that's been built to adapt as quickly as new games are released. According to Mills, "We are constantly changing and updating our system, reinventing what we are doing to keep it fresh."

The performance stats put GAME at the top of the employee engagement leaderboard, with 68% of employees accessing the platform at least twice a week and 82% believing the learning zone helps them in their day-to-day jobs. It's also making a positive impact on customer service, with 19% more praise from customers than in the past. GAME has truly earned a high score in creating something unique, aligning it with how their business operates and how their employees like to learn.

In Practice

- Think of the uniqueness of your company, your culture and your employees, and design your learning program to meet their needs directly.

A High-Touch Approach to Learning:
The Estée Lauder Companies

Situation

At the Estée Lauder Companies they have a secret ingredient for delivering outstanding service and education to create a strong emotional bond with customers, and that's through what's called a "high-touch" approach. "High-touch" is all about personalizing your approach, and going above and beyond to ensure that the customer has a satisfying and memorable experience. With this in mind, the Australian HR team set out to create an executive leadership training program, using this approach to guide them in developing and engaging leaders from across all of the company's brands.

The result has been a hugely successful program that delivers learning in a unique and creative way—inspiring and, yes, touching their current and future leaders. According to Magda Lategan,[5] Vice President HR Australia, New Zealand and South Africa, "It's been such a powerful program, creating more meaningful interactions and collaboration across all the brand teams, and at the same time helping leaders to begin to see things through a different lens."

Play

The Estée Lauder Companies' week-long residential leadership program brings together the top 50 high potential leaders from across Australia and New Zealand. Working with Macquarie Graduate School of Management, the program has been created to develop what Lategan calls "the whole person," developing their mind, their body and their spirit. Aiding this are external speakers who conduct workshops on a variety of topics that stretch the

---

[5]For a video interview with Magda, visit rg.co/magda

abilities of the participants. Past speakers have included the Wharton School's Dr. Kathy Pearson, who is an expert on strategic decision-making skills, social researcher Mark McCrindle and the Human Performance Institute's Bill McAlpine.

The daily schedule is comprehensive with all participants commencing exercise sessions at daybreak and finishing the day's workshops with guided meditation classes before embarking on evening team-building activities. Participants are taught to maintain their energy levels throughout the day with nutritious food choices, regular breaks and impromptu dance sessions—learning that they can then apply these choices to manage their energy levels and engagement in the workplace. To add to the overall learning experience, attendees are divided into learning action groups who get together each day to review their personal development goals, and discuss how they can move theory into practice.

This high-touch approach to learning and the creation of an overall experience has shown that, as with customers, the organization has also been able to create educated and engaged advocates amongst the workforce, who are loyal to their brands and passionate about leading their teams.

In Practice

- Look for ways to "touch" attendees of your learning programs through a variety of learning moments. It will help make an impact, create engagement and result in meaningful and lasting learning.

9

Recognition

Chapter Objectives

In this chapter, we will:

- Outline the problems with employee recognition as it's currently being done.
- Focus on how to improve the value you're getting from your existing recognition spend.
- Look at how to design recognition programs that truly make a difference.

Key Points

- Of the money spent on employee recognition, 87% is spent on tenure recognition—all of it wasted.
- Most companies cripple their programs with complex structures, workflows and approval processes that restrict people's abilities to just say thank you.
- To be effective, recognition has to be continuous, timely, fair, relevant and personal.
- It's the thought that counts every time; money and prizes are secondary.
- Managers and employees need training and coaching to be able to say "thank you" frequently and without fear.

Introduction

My first experience of recognition was in the early 1990s. I was 21 and in a graduate job at BT, the UK's phone company. I'd been surprised by how much of the engineering team's time was spent writing plans and reports, so I spent my evenings and weekends writing an automated documentation system to make it easier. It took four months to write, and within weeks, 45 people were using it. A month in, my boss's boss, rarely seen, told me he had nominated me for an innovation award. I was flattered—after all, I was just doing what I loved, and didn't even know there was an innovation award. But I remember feeling really great that he had noticed and thanked me.

It was over a year later, when I'd left that department, that I received a generic letter from someone I didn't know, with a gift card enclosed. I'd completely forgotten about the award by then, but the impersonal letter, combined with the realization that they'd taken a year to get it to me, left me with a negative feeling, rather than a positive one.

All in all, I felt worse than if we'd stuck to the point in the story where my boss just said thank you. It was a lesson in how poorly delivered recognition backfires, creating the exact opposite result from the one intended.

It's the Thought that Counts

Our own research found that 72% of employees felt that saying a simple "thank you" would make them feel more motivated and help build morale. That's two in every three of your employees who would be more productive if they were recognized. More at **rg.co/recognitionstats**

The Truth is Recognition Just isn't Working

In the US alone, companies are spending $46 billion per year[1] on recognition—about 2% of the total pay bill—but research shows that half of employees don't even know that a recognition program exists. Our research shows that 80% of senior leaders surveyed claim that employees are recognized monthly, but only 17% of employees think their organization's culture strongly supports recognition.

Something is really wrong with what we're doing. What, if anything, are we getting from this enormous $46 billion investment? This chapter focuses on what you can do to get your money's worth out of your recognition efforts by moving the dial to creating recognition programs that truly make a difference for your workforce and your business.

Ditch the Clocks and Watches

Recognition based on tenure, often called long-service awards, is the oldest trick in the book. Whether we're talking gold watches, engraved pens or electrical goods, it is well past its sell-by date!

Long tenure isn't a bad outcome. The problem is that spending all of your recognition money on long-service awards is a terribly ineffective way to make that happen.

Bersin & Associates finds that as much as 87%[2] of recognition spend is used for tenure awards. But have you ever worked at a company that had length of service as a company value? The harsh fact of our new world of work is that our most promising employees aren't staying in their jobs for more than a couple of

---

[1] https://www.bersin.com/News/Content.aspx?id=15543.

[2] Half of US companies use incentive programs, spending over $77 billion annually. Non-cash incentive spend is a $46 billion industry that has doubled in the last 10 years. https://www.bersin.com/News/Content.aspx?id=15543.

years, so what good is budgeting all that money for tenure awards that most of them will never reach?

We should be investing in employees who live our values and demonstrate the behaviors that build great teams, great products and loyal customers. But we're not. We're spending the money on recognizing employees equally, regardless of performance and regardless of commitment, simply based on their start dates. What we're spending on long-service awards seems like an indefensible waste of money.

Because they are predictable, long-service awards often end up becoming an entitlement: "I've worked here 15 years and this is due to me." While it needs courage to remove entitlements, since you will get a backlash, the best results we've seen are when companies divert money and time from long-service awards to performance, behavior and value awards. Running a survey can help: Ask your staff if they think you have a real culture of recognition or if you need to do more, and they will almost certainly say you need to change. That can give you the permission and the reasoning to explain to your people why you are making a bold change.

At Reward Gateway, we dropped the money from tenure awards several years ago, diverting it to a continuous recognition program based on our values. We still celebrate tenure, with e-cards sent on our social wall, allowing colleagues to shout out their favorite memories of someone and having an open dialogue about their contributions. A message, handwritten note or phone call from someone on the leadership team makes the big anniversaries special.

It's Never, Ever, Ever All about the Money

If the biggest mistake we make in recognition is tenure awards, the second-biggest mistake is to think it's all about the money. Here I want to be really clear: **It is never, ever, *ever* all about the money.**

I've seen organizations spend literally years in discussions about how much budget will be assigned to recognition awards

All of the Money Spent on Long-Service Awards Programs is Wasted

Every penny, dollar or cent you spend on tenure recognition starves the values and behavior recognition programs of funding—and they are programs that are proven to improve productivity and customer service by, on average, 14%.[3]

Tenure awards simply don't result in a culture where employees feel seen and recognized for what they've achieved and contributed. They do nothing to encourage the behaviors we need to succeed in business, and they don't make employees feel appreciated.

End them now and move the money to values- and behaviors-based recognition.

and what the process will be for signoff and approval to make sure that money goes to the right people. It's a complete waste of time. R&R, the term HR people normally use, stands for Reward & Recognition. But if we got the emphasis right, we should really be talking about *Recognition & Reward*.

A cash award, prize or gift is a *nice-to-have* for a recognition program; it can add a bit of fun and, in *some* cases, it can be motivational. But in almost every scenario I have come across, the thing that the employee values more than anything else is the *message*. The message is the part that so many organizations get wrong, and very few organizations provide any training or guidance about how to give the right message or how to recognize freely without fear.

---

[3]http://joshbersin.com/2012/06/bersin-launches-new-recognition-research-a-hidden-secret-to-talent-management/

"I have all of my important papers going back decades in a box at home. Amongst them are two handwritten thank-you notes. One is from Nick Driscombe, my ex-chairman, thanking me for a particularly good year's work. The other is from my old boss Marc Benioff at Salesforce. I'll keep those thank-you notes for ever."
—Sion Lewis, CEO Accounting at IRIS Software

The message is key. So many recognition programs spend 90% of the effort on the mechanics of the nomination or the transaction and misfire on explaining what the award is actually for, or they radically restrict the number of thank yous that can be sent to hit a budget number. Many make the process of saying thank you so arduous that few ever get round to doing it.

You can make a message more meaningful with a *thoughtful* gift, but remember that thing our parents told us when we were kids: It's the thought that counts, not the value. If you want to make a thank you more special, choose something that shows you see the recipient as a real person—a human being, not just an employee. Choose a gift or experience that shows you actually know, or have taken the time to find out, something about them.

"When you buy an experience for someone, you're thinking about them as a person, adding value and meaning to their life. The thought and meaning is worth so much more than the price you pay."
—Jack Huang, Founder & CEO at TRULY Experiences

Recognition and Visibility Go Together

It's normal to think of recognition as the corporate thank-you award program, but a key part of recognition is visibility. "Am I visible?" "Can my work be seen?" "Do other people see what I do around here?" are all key questions people ask themselves. When staff or departments complain that they are overlooked or not being recognized, it is most often the small things—the daily and hourly opportunities to acknowledge someone's work—that are being missed.

Reviewing your basic management and communication processes can be a key step in creating a high-achieving, recognition-based culture. In fact, it's important to see recognition and cross-departmental communication together. A key disengager is the feeling that the wrong people are being recognized; it creates a feeling of unfairness (see "The monkey and the cucumber" in the Pay & Benefits chapter). What's important is that recognition goes hand in hand with deliberate efforts to improve the understanding of what different departments do and how their work contributes to the mission.

> *"I've often thought I spend half my week getting people to be nicer to each other. It's not that I work with bad people; I work with wonderful people. It's just that in my experience, we are very good at seeing our own worlds as challenging and complex, but on the other hand, do a very good job of simplifying the world of others."*
> —Shelley Packer, COO at Jiminny

We noticed in our business that sales wins were celebrated most; as soon as a deal is closed, the whole company gets an e-mail and the salesperson is recognized by his or her peers. The same happens in client success, when a client buys additional services or renews a long-term contract.

But what about the success of the marketing department? And the product and engineering teams? Are they visible, too? When a salesperson wins a new client, who else was involved in crafting the winning bid? Do they highlight the whole team? Does an e-mail go to all of your managers, reflecting the totality of the talent and effort involved?

A problem in some businesses is that the same 20% of employees get recognized and the rest are starving to be noticed. Since business success is so often about the many small wins, it's important to expose your quiet achievers, your unsung heroes, giving them the recognition they deserve. Sharing those regular day-to-day achievements in a company builds social capital. It increases empathy and understanding by helping people to be kinder to each other. People can see and understand more about what others do and how they add value, and that helps inter-departmental working, collaboration and decision-making.

Don't Ration Recognition with Your Reward Budget

Recognition is not something that should be rationed; there should always be enough "thanks" to go around. Reward is the problem—that's where you will have a budget constraint. That's why you should focus 90% of your effort on recognition and only 10% on reward—the cash or monetary value part. R&R should stand for Recognition & Reward, not Reward & Recognition.

In Practice

Key Outcomes Rebels Strive For

Improved Inter-Departmental Results When sales hit their target, was it all down to the sales team or did great work between sales, service and product really land the deal?

Peer-to-peer recognition between people in different teams helps build connections across the company, resulting in improved results and lower risk. The National Transportation Safety Board found that 73% of incidents occurred on the first day a team worked together and 44% on the first flight.[4] Teams that stayed together for years performed better than the rest.

---

[4]From Margaret Heffernan's book *Beyond Measure*.

Increased Tenure   Rebels do strive for increased length of service from staff who are living their values and displaying the right behaviors—but they know that you get long tenure not by rewarding the tenure itself, but by creating an engaging workplace where people feel that they are seen, heard, recognized and valued for who they are and what they do every day. That kind of culture makes employees want to stay with you for the long term.

Key Rebel Behaviors

The classic way to build recognition programs involves budgets, committees, nominations and process. Recognition rebels really do things differently.

1. **Make recognition timely and continuous**
   Rebels build cultures of continuous recognition where saying thanks is an everyday occurrence involving peers, managers, the CEO and the whole leadership team. They move away from annual or quarterly events, recognizing that praise is more effective in the moment.
2. **Build trust**
   Rebels believe they don't need committees, complex systems and rulebooks to manage recognition programs. With recognition budgets on average less than 2% of the overall salary budget, they prioritize education over process and communication over compliance, and build self-policing recognition cultures based on trust.
3. **Link deeply to values**
   Rebels create multi-layered recognition programs, including peer-to-peer, manager and company-wide, linking them deeply to values and behaviors, showing staff that your values really count and aren't just words in the handbook.
4. **Encourage lateral recognition**
   In many companies, the relationships most in need of investment are the lateral ones between colleagues in different

departments. Rebels develop programs that enable lateral recognition, fueling the development of trust, empathy and social capital between teams. This peer-to-peer recognition is 35% more likely to have a positive impact on financial results than manager-only recognition.[5]

5. **Make recognition personal**

   When investing in gifts and incentives, rebels make them personal, using an understanding of someone as an individual to buy a meaningful gift or experience, or using technology to allow staff to share what they're saving for or would like to receive.

Making a Start

Start with Visibility   Take some time to think about the different job roles and departments in your organization. How many of your roles have results that are visible enough to be recognized: How could they or should they change? The first problem with most recognition is a lack of visibility. You'll have to address that, finding ways to see everyone, including your unsung heroes.

Communicate and Educate   Start an open conversation with your managers and leaders about recognition. Steer the conversation away from money—it's not a priority to create new recognition budgets. The most important thing that most companies can do is get rid of the fear of saying thank you and help managers see the power of prioritizing a little time for recognition every day. Many managers start out with an absolute terror of saying thank you too often, or thanking the wrong person. This must be overcome to create a culture of recognition.

---

[5]SHRM/Globoforce 2012 Employee Recognition Survey.

Implement Peer-to-Peer and Forget the Money I'm always saying there is no one-size-fits-all, but implementing non-monetary, peer-to-peer awards based on your values is as close as you're ever going to get to a universal quick win. Use technology with a social wall or sharing wall if you can, and there will be an instant uplift in your culture of recognition. The technology cost will be minimal (we know one rebel who implemented it using postcards stuck to a noticeboard).

THE PLAYS

Giving the Boot to Traditional Recognition Awards: *Venables Bell & Partners*

Situation

At Venables Bell & Partners, a San Francisco-based marketing agency, employees are not just the face or the heart and soul of the company; they are the "product, the craftsmen of what we do," says Paul Venables,[6] founder and CEO. To ensure the company's "product" (the staff) were motivated to develop the best for its clients, the agency needed to create recognition programs that would truly embrace the creativity of its craftspeople and align with the company's three values of being honest, fearless and independent.

Play

The result is a variety of recognition programs or awards that are far from traditional, taking creativity to the next level. "We believe that when it comes to our awards, it's better to be quirky, have a bit of fun and not be too corporate," says Venables.

The first example is their long-service program, or what they call the "boot award," which is given at five years of service.

---

[6]For a video interview with Paul, visit rg.co/paulvenables

Employees receive two things: a life-sized glass boot and $1,000. The catch, and what makes this different from traditional long-service awards, is that the money is not for the individual; it's to be used for others in the company. Whether it's picking up the tab at a local bar, taking team members out for a bit of 1:1 coaching or pooling award money to take a group out for a meal, the intent is to use it for others. "It's a way for the veterans to share what they know, carry on the culture and build relationships across the company. It creates cross-pollination, sharing with the wide-eyed and hungry youngsters what it takes to succeed," says Venables.

Another example are awards given out at the annual holiday party. They've been developed to recognize employees for their contributions, doing so again in a fun and quirky way.

- **Golden toilet:** given to the employee who "takes care of shit gracefully and with class," says Venables; the awardee receives a full-size golden toilet.
- **Multiplier:** given to the employee where everything they touch gets so much better, doubling their salary for a month.
- **Ass-kicker of the year:** given to an accomplished kicker-of-asses who gets things done; the awardee receives a bonus check.
- **Spouse/partner/significant other:** since the agency always includes significant others at key events despite the expense doubling, this award is given not to employees, but to the significant other for their support; they receive a weekend away for two at a spa, complete with babysitting services.

The final example is the **Fearless project** award, which links directly back to the agency's second value of being fearless. Employees pitch ideas for fearless projects and the entire workforce selects the winner, who receives $15,000 to go out and do their project, with the responsibility of sharing the outcome and experience.

These programs have made a difference in the motivation and engagement of the agency's workforce. In three years, staff turnover is down 75% and remains way below the industry average. Over a quarter of the staff have been employed for five years or more, and the agency has experienced double-digit revenue growth every year in that timeframe. "Our culture is everything," says Venables. "I have faith that if we can cultivate the right culture, it will attract and retain the right people, and they will in turn do the right kind of work."

In Practice

- Consider alternative approaches for rewarding long service, especially those that engage the recipient and others in the company.
- Don't be afraid to be a bit creative in the awards you use to recognize your employees—a little originality can go far in engaging your workforce.

Recognizing an Offline Workforce: *ICC Sydney*

Situation

ICC Sydney is an exhibition and convention center in Australia that is dedicated to bringing extraordinary experiences to its visitors. The same holds true for the workforce, with an Employee Value Proposition (EVP) saying, "Together we do the extraordinary."

With this focus on people and on the "extraordinary," the company decided to put in place recognition programs to thank the workforce for their dedication and reward them for their efforts. The challenge was: How can you do this for an operational workforce, where only 20% sit in front of the computer, with the remainder working out in the venues? How do you create something that is equal for everyone?

Play

The answer for ICC Sydney was to create not just one recognition program but three, helping to meet their objectives in a variety of ways.

- **Checkbooks**
  People leaders are given physical checkbooks from the "Bank of Extraordinary," which act as instant recognition for everyday achievements. Checks can be given out by leaders as well as by peers, with leader approval, to employees who demonstrate behaviors in line with company values. These checks, which come in $5, $10 and $20 denominations, can be redeemed for gifts or banked to save for larger gifts. There's a wide and interesting selection, ranging from a bottle of wine to movie tickets, to having your house cleaned.
- **The Extraordinaires**
  The Extraordinaires is ICC Sydney's annual recognition program, with winners nominated and selected by peers. There are nine categories—three based on ICC Sydney values, three based on their EVP and three aligned to the business. Winners are selected by a panel of employees representing all levels within the company, who vote based on specific selection criteria. Crystal engraved trophies are awarded and photos are taken to hang on a special wall, giving the employee and others something to remember long after the award ceremony.
- **Golden Ticket**
  The Golden Ticket award can only be awarded by the CEO, and is done in special circumstances when an employee has gone above and beyond. A recent award example is an office

employee who heard on the radio that a fire had started at an exhibition and ran down and put it out, going above and beyond to manage the situation. The award is a choice between an extra day of vacation or a stay at a five-star hotel with their partner.

Together these awards highlight, recognize and reward employees for truly being extraordinary. "It is only through the extraordinary efforts of our team that we can deliver extraordinary events. Reward and recognition has been the cornerstone of our success and has been the key ingredient to bring our HR programs together,"says Mathew Paine.[7]

In Practice

- Recognition can happen even with an offline workforce, so overcome any challenges you may have, and build recognition at your company.
- Recognition can and should come from the top, so make sure your CEO is a key part of your recognition program and culture.

A Recognition Program that Will Make You Smile: *Hershey Company*

Situation

Go to the Hershey Company's website and you'll find that it says, "We've been bringing goodness to the world, one smile, one moment and one person at a time." In 2013, the company's engagement survey found a decline in how employees felt they

---

[7]For a video interview with Mathew, visit rg.co/mathewpaine

were being recognized, which opened up an opportunity to deliver on the company's mission better. What could the team do to bring smiles back to the faces of employees?

The answer was to design a new global recognition program, called, aptly, Hershey "SMILES". Since the program's been in place, it's outperformed expectations with an increase in employee engagement scores of 23% (14 basis points) over a three-year period. The program is so much a part of the company and the culture that, as Cesar Villa, Director of Total Rewards, says, "One employee is recognized every seven minutes." That's a lot of smiles!

Play

Before putting SMILES in place, Hershey's had different recognition programs in 26 countries, so its 18,000 employees were having different recognition experiences. SMILES, which is now delivered to all employees globally in five languages and is based on the company's global behaviors, provides a combination of both consistency (one program and one platform) and flexibility (six recognition levels to choose from).

The six recognition levels range from a simple thank you to a financial award in the amount of $250 (or local equivalents). "We started with four levels, but found we needed additional levels to award for specific situations," says Villa. To ensure levels are selected in a consistent way, the recognition platform asks five questions, leading the person requesting the award to the right level, and provides additional tips and training.

To work alongside the SMILES program, two other programs support the renewed culture of recognition. The first is a quarterly social recognition called "Remarkable People," a program to highlight employees who have been recognized during a specific time period. The second is the "Milton Hershey Award for Excellence," which is an annual celebration to recognize remarkable successes across all areas of the business. Together, these programs drive employee engagement and link to the company mission by recognizing one person at a time, bringing one smile after another.

In Practice

- When selecting the name for your recognition program, create one that is meaningful, easy to remember and can be used globally.
- Don't underestimate the power of thanks as well as simple, low-cost recognition awards. They are and can be just as effective as those that are more costly.

Adding a ThankMe to Your Recognition Program: *Coleman Group*

Situation

When Joanne Sullivan,[8] Corporate Social Responsibility Director, moved from the hospitality to the demolition sector, she saw some immediate opportunities. She had seen first-hand the power of recognition with hospitality customers and employees, and wanted to bring this to Coleman to overcome the challenges of engaging with a workforce dispersed across 10 moving work-sites who demolish big and complicated buildings. She developed an innovative and cost-effective recognition program that increased employee engagement from 60% to 82% in just one year. That's a huge achievement at any company, but even more so since she had to win over the hearts and minds of a workforce unaccustomed to recognition.

---

[8]For a video interview with Joanne, visit rg.co/joannesullivan

Play

When Sullivan first went to the business with her recognition ideas, they "just stared at me, and said that no one would like them." She decided to give it a go anyway, and introduced "Wacky Wednesday", which involved sending each site a box containing old-fashioned games and sweets. Sullivan said it was hit and miss, but when she asked for feedback, ideas rolled in for the next event, so next they did a "Quiz Week", posting questions on the company's online intranet each day relating to business and company values, with teams winning prizes for the best answers.

These smaller events grew into "ThankMe Week", which now takes place twice a year. It's the company's way to "genuinely say thank you," says Sullivan, with a new activity launched on the intranet daily. Recently, one of these weeks included "Munchy Monday", where each site bought breakfast for employees; "Time Off Tuesday", where an employee's name was picked every hour to get their birthday off; "RewardMe Wednesday", where employees won cash prizes through the company's discounts portal; "ThankMe Thursday", where senior leaders created and posted a video to thank employees for their efforts and contributions; and "FreeTime Friday", where all employees could go home two hours early.

According to Sullivan, "We plan it well in advance so it doesn't affect day-to-day activities, and give managers a month's notice to plan their workloads." This is extremely important, since 70% of their workforce works for clients offsite, and the business wants all employees to have the same experience. "We've had to get creative," says Sullivan, but employees have helped the HR team come up with new ideas to keep the week fresh and effective. This works, along with peer-to-peer e-cards and manager instant awards, which empowers managers to give small cash awards to employees with no approval required. Together, these programs create a culture where employees feel appreciated 365 days a year.

In Practice

- Look for opportunities to add simple, fun and low-cost activities to your recognition program.
- If you struggle with getting leadership buy-in, see if you can do something small and simple to build trust and support before going big.

Recognition that "Crushes It": *SnackNation*

Situation

SnackNation, a office snack delivery service, had been holding a "Crush It Call" every Friday at 4 p.m. since the company was founded. The entire team would form a circle, go around the room one by one and recognize someone who had "crushed it"—gone above and beyond in a way that exemplified the company's core values—and then name one thing they were grateful for. It had become a signature part of the company culture, embodying the desire to "shine a light on the accomplishments and every-day victories that might otherwise go unsung," according to Jeff Murphy, Director of Communications.

But then something happened: The company grew. With more than 100 people, it simply took too long to go around the circle. Was it time to give up on the tradition, or did the company need to find a way to keep it alive? Luckily, the company chose the latter, and evolved the Crush It Call to achieve the same effect, while still meeting the needs of the growing business. It's contributed to the company being named to *Entrepreneur* magazine's Top Company Culture in 2017, and by the *LA Business Journal* as one of the Best Places to Work in Los Angeles.

Play

The company first tried a technology-driven approach to accommodate the growing team, with employees posting their Crushes on a digital portal. Automatic e-mails were sent directly to the person being recognized, with a running feed of Crushes for the entire company to see at any point in time.

The digital version of the Crush It Call left out something essential, though: The element of human connection. "To us, giving a Crush is like giving someone a gift," says SnackNation co-founder and CEO Sean Kelly.[9] "And giving someone a gift is much more special in person than virtually."

Eventually, the Crush It Call went back to its in-person roots, but this time on a voluntary basis and with a 30-minute time limit. While everyone still attends, only those who volunteer present their Crush. They also end with a company leader speaking on a specific weekly theme, helping the team see the bigger picture of what was accomplished and what should be celebrated. It's a good way to maintain the human element while making the program feasible with such a large group.

"The Crush It Call is arguably more important now than ever before," Kelly explains. "Besides facilitating team bonding and sending everyone into the weekend with smiles on their faces, the practice helps break down the siloes that can develop as organizations grow. It also helps give everyone a more holistic understanding of the business, and inspires new avenues for collaboration."

In Practice

- Find ways to continue your recognition traditions as you grow, leveraging technology to help you achieve this.
- Never underestimate the impact of face-to-face recognition, which can inspire and create collaboration amongst teams.

---

[9]For a video interview with Sean, visit rg.co/seankelly

Building Your Recognition Pyramid: *Homeserve*

Situation

Homeserve, a home emergency repair business, had a recognition program that had worked fine over the years, but as the business grew, it had "lost some direction, with employees not feeling recognized and with a lack of consistency," according to Liz Crutchley,[10] Head of Reward and Benefits. The company decided to develop a new recognition strategy, one with a very straightforward objective of "keeping it effortless," which aligned with HomeServe's customer-first service approach.

It has been highly successful, helping Homeserve increase employee engagement from 56% to 82% over the last three years, as well as earning recognition itself, ranking third on Glassdoor's Best Places to Work after never having been on the list in the past. In addition, Homeserve also made the list of Bloomberg's Best UK Employers.

Play

The new recognition strategy, "Special Thanks and Recognition" (STAR awards), was developed using a pyramid approach, creating four levels of recognition to engage and recognize employees against the company's people behaviors.

The first level is anytime e-cards, where employees at any level can send e-cards delivering a simple message of thank you. The next level is "Above and Beyond" awards (bronze, silver, gold and diamond), with increasing financial value ranging from specific demonstration of one of the people behaviors through demonstrable performance to help the business achieve its strategic goals. Anyone can be nominated, with senior managers approving and then awarding employees money to be spent through the company's online employee discount platform.

---

[10]For a video interview with Liz, visit rg.co/lizcrutchley

The third level sees all those who received gold and diamond awards put forward for a Quarterly award, with public recognition to showcase their contributions and additional financial rewards through the discount platform.

Finally, for the Annual award, the best of the best are selected from quarterly award winners and invited to a memorable award event and receive praise and recognition from the executive team for their significant contributions and to celebrate their accomplishments.

The theme throughout the four levels goes back to Homeserve's initial objective, which was "keeping it effortless." Each and every program is easy to understand and easy to use. It must be working, since the company's 3,000 employees sent more than 22,000 e-cards and more than 5,000 STAR awards in one year alone.

In Practice

- When developing your recognition strategy, consider creating different levels/plans to build a recognition pyramid for your company.
- Think of your audience, making recognition simple and effortless. The more you do this, the more your employees will engage with your programs.

Making Your Employees Feel Like Stars: *Virgin Group*

Situation

For more than five decades, the Virgin brand has been recognized for providing a "unique and exceptional customer experience," whether that's in its banking, travel, entertainment, health and fitness, or communications business. All of it is accomplished through the company's brand values of "delightfully surprising, red hot, and straight up."

How does this translate into a group-wide recognition program and event? How would Virgin create an annual recognition tradition to bring the group together, celebrate and recognize amazing employees from all over the world, creating the excitement and buzz that Virgin delivers to customers?

The answer? "Virgin Stars of the Year", which is one of the major highlights of the Virgin calendar. As more businesses have joined the Virgin family, the reward has grown from a simple dinner with founder Sir Richard Branson and his family to an event that could give the Oscars a run for their money.

Play

During the year, recognition is left up to the individual businesses, but when it comes to annual recognition, that is done at the Virgin Group level with the Star of the Year event. About 50 employees are selected from the 71,300 staffers around the world for bringing the Virgin brand to life, and brought to London for what Samantha Smart, People Strategy Business Partner, calls "a once-in-a-lifetime magical experience."

There's magic in everything surrounding the program, whether it's the event itself or how employees are recognized. The event always has a theme; a recent one was "Willy Wonka meets Alice in Wonderland." The team brought the theme to life by serving cocktails in teacups, having a golden gate and having no other than Sir Richard Branson greeting attendees dressed as Willy Wonka. The awards, besides bringing awardees to London (many for the very first time), gave recipients goody bags brimming with gifts from different brands. Awardees also had their pictures taken with Branson and, finally, actually had stars named after them.

Besides delivering against the objective of making employees feel valued and appreciated, and giving them a once-in-a-lifetime experience, the awards also have been proven to increase retention, increase engagement and increase employee net promoter scores (eNPS). And why not—a night like this would certainly make anyone feel like a star!

In Practice

- Find your own way to bring magic to your recognition programs. Whether it's day-to-day, quarterly or annual, sprinkle magic dust every way you can.

- Remember that recognition isn't about the money. Experiences like this will be valued, remembered and talked about more than cash recognition awards.

10

Pay & Benefits

Chapter Objectives

In this chapter, we will:

- Discuss pay and incentives focusing heavily on fairness and transparency.
- Look at a simple model that explains the four reasons benefits can add value for you.
- Highlight how the complexity of benefits hampers communication and uptake.

Key Points

- Many issues with pay are about fairness. The "monkey and the cucumber" experiment tells you almost everything you need to know.
- Pay is rarely private and is becoming less so, meaning unfairness gets uncovered more frequently and faster than ever.
- Cash is the most expensive way to pay someone. Effective benefits should amplify employer money.
- Creative use of benefits is key to building an Employee Value Proposition (EVP) that helps you stand out.

Introduction

Pay and benefits on their own cannot create engagement and must be used as part of a broader effort involving several elements of the Engagement Bridge™ model. That does not mean they are unimportant—pay is a key disengager, especially if not handled fairly, and benefits can have a positive impact because they are highly visible and tangible. They can serve as a quick-and-easy first move when starting to build a more engaging culture; a bit like offering an olive branch to your workforce to say, "Hey, we're here, we value you and we want to start a better relationship." They're also a tangible and publicly visible signpost to your culture—as long as you follow through with the rest of the Bridge™.

Pay

We could focus an entire book on pay strategies and practices, but I'd prefer to to focus on pay and its direct effect on employee engagement. Interestingly, there is no correlation between how much you are paid and how engaged you are: **You can be engaged or disengaged wherever you are on the career ladder.**

Pay is a Brutal Disengager and Demotivator

Let's start by getting the elephant out in the open. **Pay is never a positive force on engagement**. Life would be easier if it were, but you just can't buy people like that—not many people anyway. You can never create engagement by paying people more. There can be a fleeting motivational and feel-good factor, but it dissipates as fast as the ink dries on the pay review letter. However, you can destroy or disable engagement in a blink of an eye using pay, although not quite in the way you might think.

If we think back to our Chapter 1 definition of what an engaged employee is, then it's clear that paying someone more money can have no positive or lasting impact on their buy-in to the mission, understanding of how their role contributes to that mission, and urge to see the company win and succeed. **Pay, in isolation, cannot buy engagement; it never did and never will.**

The Monkey and the Cucumber

Probably everything you need to know about how people think about and act in terms of pay is shown in "The Monkey and the Cucumber" experiment.[1]

Only Some of Our People are Money-Motivated

We make a mistake if we think that *all* our people are motivated by money and are out to selfishly maximize their lot in life. The truth is that only *some* people prioritize money in that way. Many more are driven by an aversion to inequity—a fancy term for a strong preference for fairness.

"The Monkey and the Cucumber" experiment shows that capuchin monkeys have the same aversion to inequity as humans. In this 4-minute video, two monkeys are trained to hand over pebbles in exchange for a piece of cucumber. Both do so quite happily, until one monkey is given a grape: a sweeter, higher-value treat. The other monkey, who seconds ago was perfectly happy with the cucumber, reacts immediately and dramatically by throwing the cucumber back at the researcher and rattling the side of the cage to voice her anger at the unfairness of this inequity.

---

[1]Brosnan, Sarah F., and de Waal, Frans B.M. 2003. "Monkeys reject unequal pay."

To see the video go to rg.co/monkey

I've seen this happen first-hand many times. You have some-one totally engaged—loving their job; completely happy with pay, benefits and everything else—and then the next day, discon-nected, feeling cheated, and believing the company doesn't value them or recognize their contributions. What happened between these two days? A recruiter saying, "Hey, it's not fair what they're paying you. You're really worth twice that." Often the job being referred to isn't remotely comparable, but it still creates a strong enough sense of unfairness to seriously unsettle someone.

There are data showing this link. Kronos and Future Workplace surveyed 614 US HR professionals in a study on employee burnout and found that "unfair compensation" was the top contributor to stress, 25% ahead of "unreasonable workload" and "too much after-hours work."[2] It seems that unfairness cre-ates an emotional response that is hard to ignore.

Incentives and Performance-related Pay Can Make It Worse

Among the biggest contributors to disengagement are incentives and performance-related pay. As the monkey and the cucumber taught us, when one employee thinks they deserve more, you'll inevitably wind up with more and more parts of the business

---

[2]https://www.kronos.com/about-us/newsroom/employee-burnout-crisis-study-reveals-big-workplace-challenge-2017.

demanding incentives. The problem is that this leads to management "hearing the noise" and thinking their people will work harder if they're incentivized, but it's actually an issue of fairness and equity. Let's look at a typical sales team as a common example.

Most sales teams are paid on a bonus or commission arrangement, despite some good bodies of evidence that actually only some salespeople are coin-operated in the way we think they all are.[3]

This works fine until someone in the service team who handles client renewals feels it's unfair because *they* don't get a commission. We fix that by inventing a commission program for them, which works fine until a product manager thinks it's unfair because they get nothing even though they created the product.

We fix that by giving the product manager some sort of performance target for product sales—and another slice of commission. This works until ... well, you get the idea. The vicious circle continues, with more and more incentive programs being created, each one adding to the inequity rather than solving it.

Take Care with Incentives

Badly designed incentives can turn connected business processes into disconnected silos. These can literally drive people apart, rather than harnessing and rewarding their efforts.

The irony of it all is that 90% of the people involved weren't actually motivated by money anyway: They didn't need the extrinsic reward. They were motivated to demand a correction to the unfairness—the inequity of being given a cucumber when someone next to them was given a grape. The real tragedy is that there is significant evidence that bringing in an extrinsic reward actually destroys the existing intrinsic drivers.[4]

---

[3]For more in-depth detail read *Drive* by Daniel Pink or our summary at **rg.co/ coinoperated**.

[4]Daniel Pink's book

There's No Hiding from Pay Transparency   Whether we like it or not, salaries are becoming more transparent, which increases the chance that unfair (or even fair) treatment will be unearthed. Sites like Glassdoor, Salary.com and Payscale all run open-pay benchmarking that is directly available to employees, openly and without subscription. Much of this information is taken out of context or without enough details, but our employees are seeing and believing it, which can cause real issues.

With pay becoming more transparent and unfairness proven as a key disengager, it's clear that if you want to build a resilient bridge with your people, you'll have to get started on prioritizing fairness.

The only real option we have is to start a culture of more openness about pay: discussing the benchmarks—explaining what we think of them honestly and why they are or are not relevant.

Most Staff Actually Want Pay Transparency

Glassdoor's Global Salary Transparency Survey found that 70% of employees believed pay transparency would be good for employee satisfaction, and a similar number thought it would improve performance, but only 36% of employees said their companies disclosed salary levels openly.[5]

A few companies have figured out how to tackle this challenge of fairness—being true rebels by pioneering a bold approach to pay transparency. They make pay public for everyone to see; whether it's individual salaries, pay ranges or pay formulas used, they've raised the curtain on pay. An example is the US grocery

---

[5]See rg.co/gdsurvey2016

chain Whole Foods, which made all salaries public, right up to the CEO, as part of its team-first collaborative culture. Another example is Buffer, which was featured in Chapter 3.

Benefits are Here to Benefit your Company and Your Employees

Every now and again, I'll meet someone who will proudly tell me that they don't believe in benefits and all they give their staff is salary. My reply is always the same: "You must be wealthy then, because you're wasting a load of money—you're paying staff in the most expensive way: cash." That normally gets enough interest for me to explain why a cost-effective, well-rounded Employee Value Proposition (EVP), which looks at the entire proposition, should always have a strong and healthy benefits provision.

Good benefits are, on the whole, an *amplifier* of employer money. When we provide a benefit to staff, it's normally because we believe the perceived value of that benefit is greater than the cost to us to provide. Sometimes the amplification is caused by a tax benefit created by the government; very commonly, it's created by the bulk or pool-buying ability of an employer. Some of the most effective benefits, such as discount programs, can increase employee net income by up to 10% while costing less than 0.1% of payroll.

Salary is the Most Expensive Way to Pay People

Effective benefits amplify employer money because they cost less than the perceived value to the employee. Smart employers move money from the pay budget to the benefits budget to fund big-impact programs without drastically increasing overall costs.

Whether you're buying health or other insurances, legal services such as writing a will, or financial advice, you're paying less for it as an employer than if the employees had to buy it themselves. If you're not, then frankly, just give the employees the extra salary and let them have the choice of buying it themselves. Unless, that is, it fits into categories 2, 3 or 4, making you *want* to provide it.

Category	Reason to provide[6]
1. Economic	**Helps employees save money and amplifies employer spend** Examples: health care, insurances, discounts on products, gyms, childcare costs
2. Cultural	**Makes a statement about your company culture or drives a behavior you want** Examples: wellbeing allowance or subsidized gym membership to support or create a culture where wellness is encouraged/supported
3. Time	**Helps employees save time** Examples: on-site dry cleaning, food or other concierge services to maximize time at work
4. Regulatory	**Provided because they are required by law/legislation** Example: retirement plans, paid vacation

Sometimes a benefit may fit into more than one of these categories, and that's fine. At Reward Gateway's London office, our staff cafeteria provides a subsidized healthy lunch. This saves our staff time from going out, is a positive wellbeing action and amplifies employer money because the cost of running the café is less than the cost of our staff eating out every day. The benefits to be wary of are those that fit in none of the boxes.

Put Benefits Complexity on the Shelf

Benefits are only valuable if they are *known about, understood and valued by employees.*

---

[6]Benefits that you provide because you think you have to to be competitive with other employers still originate in one of these four categories.

The vast majority of companies do much better at procuring new benefits than they do in communicating them and making them accessible. They then wonder why only 5% of their employees actually uses them or why benefits are not valued.

Organizations have to change their approach to benefit communication completely if they're going to engage with their workforces, especially their millennials. HR has to keep in mind that employees struggle to cope with the complexity, concepts and terminology used in benefit plans, especially ones such as retirement and insurance.

Companies struggle with communicating benefits, but not due to a lack of care or prioritization. The problem is underestimating the sheer scale of the task when some benefits are so incredibly complex. Reducing complexity in the benefits themselves, which means biting the bullet and asking whether the complexity is really necessary, is actually an essential step to making effective benefits communications even possible.

Too Complex to Explain?

When considering introducing a new benefit or an additional tier or option, think about how it will be presented to employees and whether you can explain it clearly. Ask yourself whether the additional complexity is necessary and if you need to simplify something else to make room for the messages.

Rebels are turning benefits communication into things people really want to receive, rather than want to avoid. They leverage the marketing department, external agencies and social media to sell benefits like the company sells products: Focusing on simple and engaging key messages.

In Practice

Key Outcomes Rebels Strive for

Getting pay & benefits right is hugely important because it's a key underpinning element to the Engagement Bridge™.

Pay & Benefits Aligned to Culture   The starting point for any pay & benefit decisions must be a clear and compelling strategy aligned to culture and the company values. This creates focus and alignment so all programs work together as part of your overall EVP.

Pay & Benefits that Fit into the Wider Package   Keep in mind that pay & benefits are only part of your overall engagement package, and for that reason, must sit alongside other elements of the Bridge™ to be effective. Think of how they all add up, connecting and working together.

Improved Trust   Alongside other elements of the Bridge™, pay & benefits can go a long way toward building and maintaining trust with your workforce. They show that that you value your employees by treating them fairly, with consideration and compassion.

Key Rebel Behaviors

Rebels with high-performing cultures behave differently from normal companies in the following ways.

1. **Prioritize fairness in pay**
   Rebels tackle pay fairness head on by using pay budgets to address pay inconsistencies, making sure salaries are fair and can be justified. They find ways to move to a more open and

transparent approach to pay, whether it's starting by sharing pay philosophies, pay ranges or a fully transparent approach of sharing salaries. Remember that regardless of company policy, people do talk and share, so be ready to deal with this proactively.

2. **Replace incentive pay with company-wide programs**
   Rebels replace team and role-specific incentives with better management, coaching and development. They design jobs where people are accountable and can see their results outside of a pay plan. They lean strongly on profit sharing and all-staff programs as a way of creating ownership and turning employees into stakeholders, deeply connected to the financial success of the business.

3. **Use benefits as a cultural differentiator**
   Rebels match their peers on core benefits—but then go much further, looking for creative opportunities to show their personalities and that they're different. They're unafraid to invent benefits themselves and are unconstrained by what's available to purchase from third parties. They build on this unique provision through other parts of the Bridge™, often connecting benefits to mission, values and recognition.

4. **Use benefits to maximize value**
   Rebels understand that good benefits outperform cash in terms of value for money, visibility and in the cultural statement that they make. They see pay & benefits as a single budget, allowing money to flow between them, understanding that when benefits are chosen well and implemented well, they amplify employer money.

5. **Develop a culture of benefits flexibility**
   Rebels stand out by creating a culture that allows iteration, review and change. Established HR thinking is that it is really hard to withdraw benefits after they've been launched.

Rebels overcome with techniques like branding benefits as "Our benefits for this year," involving employees in feedback and review, sharing uptake statistics openly, and making changes—often while explaining what was swapped for what and why.

Making a Start

Get Employee Input and Feedback   To get employees to provide input and feedback, announce to your staff that you're reviewing your benefits. Tell them your goal is clear: You want to understand which benefits they value so you can create a more meaningful and relevant benefits package. Explain that that the purpose is not to save money. Engage with them.

Try focus groups, surveys or technology, which allow staff to make suggestions for other staff to vote and comment on. Set expectations at the start of the review that you'll make changes and some benefits will get replaced, and start building an expectation that change is good and normal.

Look for Low-cost or No-cost Benefits   Options will differ based on your company's size and context, but look for new benefits that will create value yet don't cost a lot. Examples include small wedding or baby bonuses, a free staff lottery, early closing on Friday, a full or half-day off for birthdays, time off for volunteering, or a shopping or restaurant discount program. See more at **rg.co/benefitsideas**.

Build in Balance and Choice   We have five generations in the workplace these days, so if you don't have balance in your benefit offering, you won't have benefits that appeal to each generation. Your younger staff do not get excited by the idea of a retirement plan; they're more interested in saving money on all their new clothes or going out on the town. By creating a balanced benefit offering, you'll have something for every generation.

THE PLAYS

Benefits That Truly Meet the Needs of your Workforce: *Goodman Masson*

Situation

Guy Hayward, Goodman Masson's CEO, set himself and his financial recruitment business a lofty strategic goal: To treat their people not just well, but "better than any other business in the UK." Recognizing that a key component for achieving this was through benefits, they set out to develop a package that would work for their 140-strong, mainly millennial, workforce. The result was a benefits package that's won numerous awards; a company that's won "Best Recruitment Company to Work For" and "Great Place to Work" honors; and increased profits, engagement and retention.

Play

The package Goodman Masson put in place is called "Benefits Boutique", and it contains a varied and unique offering. It was developed by "reflecting on and considering the modern-day challenges that our people face, looking at how each benefit would fit their lifestyle and helping to improve their standard of living," says Hayward.

An example is the mortgage fund, which allows employees to build up a deposit for a first property. Employees deposit a portion of their salary/bonus over a three-year period and at the end, the company adds an additional 50% of salary and 33% for bonus contributions made. Roughly 25% of employees have joined the fund, and three have even bought their first properties. "There's a different bond and feel toward Goodman Masson as an employer," says Andrew Michael, Managing Director. "Even if an employee is not in the fund, knowing they work for an organization that is that giving and is that generous creates a different feel."

Other examples are loan programs, which include a student loan, a home improvement loan, a new-parent loan and even an exotic holiday loan. For all, the company pays the upfront costs, with the employee repaying through payroll deductions spread over 12 to 18 months. This is highly valued by employees because it means they can do things they may not have been able to afford, or save money by not having to take out high-interest loans.

The development of this package has been a gradual process, with new elements being offered over the years, based on a constant review of asking "What else can we do?" "The overarching aim is finding ways to take the financial strain and pressure off the shoulders of our employees, supporting them in leading more productive and rewarding lives both in and out of the workplace," says Michael.

In Practice

- Look for opportunities to introduce benefits specifically targeting the needs of your workforce.
- Recognize the financial stress your workforce is facing. Are there ways you can support them through programs or education?
- Consider benefits involving loans. These are interesting: They use up a small amount of company cash flow and require a limited amount of administration, but otherwise have no costs. As long as you manage leavers correctly, you can use your company's spare cash flow to create high-value, zero-cost benefits.

Sometimes All It Takes is an Ice Cream Van: *PhlexGlobal*

Situation

At PhlexGlobal, a global provider of electronic document management systems and services to the clinical research sector, what employees do is critical to the successful creation of new drugs.

However, since it is in a highly regulated industry, much of the work for many of the staff is routine and repetitive. PhlexGlobal wanted to find ways to let its workforce know they were valued, along with new ways to engage employees.

Play

PhlexGlobal's approach to engagement is to put in place what I'd call "surprise benefits"—those that no one expects, but when provided, are hugely engaging. One example is having a local ice cream van park at the office to surprise and delight employees with free ice cream. Many companies give out free ice cream, either in the cafeterias or buying boxes to hand out on a hot day, but what makes this special is that it was unexpected, and it turned an inexpensive ice cream into a memorable experience. As the van arrived, the musical chimes put a smile on faces and everyone had fun hanging outside with colleagues.

Other examples used from time to time include scattering Easter eggs on desks from the "Easter Bunny" or giving employees a half-day off for some much-needed holiday shopping. As Stella Donoghue, previous Managing Director at PhlexGlobal, said, "You don't need to spend a lot of money or do something big to engage your workforce. We've had great results by putting a bit of fun and surprise in what we've done. It's not always what you do, but how you do it, that matters."

In Practice

- Do something simple, fun and spontaneous for your workforce. It truly will make a difference, and be something they'll talk about and engage with.

Creating a Fair and Transparent Approach to Pay: *Basecamp*

Situation

Basecamp produces software that allows a company to bring multiple projects together into one project management tool. Doing this acts as one central source of truth and makes things clear so everyone in the company knows what to do.

Basecamp's pay model has a similar aim of adding clarity and truths to an area that is surrounded in mystery in many companies. According to Jason Fried, co-founder and CEO, "Hiring and training people is not only expensive, but draining. All that energy could go into making better products with people you've kept happy for the long term by being fair and transparent about pay & benefits. There's a fountain of happiness and productivity in working with a stable crew. I'm baffled such a competitive advantage isn't more diligently sought."

Play

Basecamp's approach to being fair and transparent with pay has many levels, which is what makes it both unique and effective. Starting with base pay, there are no negotiated salaries or pay raises. Everyone in the same role at the same level is paid the same salary. "Equal work, equal pay," says Fried. This is true regardless of where employees work in the US, with target pay set at the top 5% of its Chicago headquarter market rates; whether employees live in California, Alaska or Illinois, they're paid the same salary. "This means everyone has the freedom to pick where they want to live, with no penalty for relocating to a cheaper cost-of-living area. We encourage remote working and have many employees who've lived all over while continuing to work for Basecamp," says Fried.

The next area where Basecamp displays its unique approach is with bonuses, which they don't pay, but instead are built into base salaries. "We used to pay bonuses many years ago, but found they were quickly treated as expected salary anyway," says Fried. Instead, a profit-growth sharing program shares 25% of annual total profit growth with employees, which they believe sets fewer expectations.

Finally, there are no stock options at Basecamp, but that's only because they never intend to sell the company. However, being fair and transparent again, they've vowed to employees that should they sell the company, they'll distribute 5% of the proceeds to all current employees.

This approach to pay has helped Basecamp maintain an engaged and stable workforce with an average tenure of five years in an industry where companies are lucky to have employees stay for two years. Basecamp's approach shows engagement comes from fairness and respect, not sky-high salaries or millionaire stock options.

In Practice

- Look at what you're trying to achieve with your pay programs, and make sure they're helping you achieve this and not getting in your way. For example, do complicated geographic pay structures create fairness or prevent your workforce from moving to where you may need them to work?

A Participative Approach to Pay: *Semler*

Situation

Ricardo Semler, previous CEO of Semler, a Brazilian industrial machinery company, is famous for his unorthodox approach to running a business. In his book *Maverick*, he explains the journey taken from moving the business he took over from his father that was run traditionally to one run in a participative way; or, as he says in his book, "A more humane, trusting, productive, exhilarating, and, in every sense, rewarding way."

This participative approach is evident in the way salaries are set and profits are distributed through the company's profit-sharing program, with employees playing an active role. These approaches, and many others relating to programs and policies, continue to be radical 25 years after the book was published. Were they successful? Based on Semler's new approach, the company had one of the highest growth rates in Brazil, despite large multinationals entering the market and savage recessions.

Play

During the first years of Semler's journey into participative management, the company involved employees in a variety of decisions, setting the direction and foundation for the approaches to pay to follow. The first involved their profit-sharing plan: The company created one that employees not only understood but controlled, letting the beneficiaries make the decisions. This included negotiating with employees on how much of the profits would be shared, educating them on financials so numbers wouldn't be picked out of the air. They also worked with employees to decide how profits would be divided, letting each location vote on how this was done.

Next came a "self-set" pay approach, letting nearly 25% of the employees set their own salaries. The process begins with employees completing an evaluation form, helping them focus on their roles and their value. In addition, before suggesting what they believe they should be paid, employees are asked to consider four criteria: What they think they could make elsewhere, what others with similar responsibilities and skills make at Semler, what friends with similar backgrounds make, and how much money they need to live. To support this process, the company shares salaries, as well as pay surveys, with employees.

These non-traditional approaches—ones that challenge our ways of doing business—have helped Semler succeed in good times and bad. They've eliminated complaints about pay, and have shown other companies a different, more inclusive way of running a company.

In Practice

- Find ways to hear your employees' voice when making pay decisions—gaining their perspectives and views can improve both decision-making and acceptance.
- Find ways to share information relating to financials and pay so employees have a better understanding of the business and what underlies pay decisions.

Using Sporting Events to Reward Employees: *McDonald's*

Situation

Like many companies, McDonald's was looking for ways to reward outstanding performance by using incentives. As a long-standing sponsor of the FIFA World Cup, they decided to use the sporting event as a way to do this with its employees, which at the time numbered more than 85,000, spread across 1,200 restaurants. The incentive program combined a love of sport with a love of customer service and, as the results show, delivered on "scoring" with both groups.

Play

The incentive program, called "Road to Rio", was based on that year's World Cup location, and incentivized the top 5% of restaurants based on customer satisfaction and speed of service rankings over the three months leading up to the event. Each of these top restaurants received a hamper full of chocolate for employees to share, and was then entered into a draw to win one of 11 trips to the World Cup for the restaurant manager and a cash prize to be used for an employee social event at the restaurant.

Employees weren't the only winners: The competition was designed by the National Operations team to boost the speed of service while still delivering a great customer experience. The average service time in restaurants improved by more than 6 seconds compared to the previous year, and the customer satisfaction score also improved.

According to Neal Blackshire, UK Reward Manager at the time, "The combined improvement in satisfaction and speed means that we delivered a great customer experience to an additional 24,000 customers every day. This was a marked improvement and helped to create a real buzz in the restaurants. We were delighted to be able to give our employees the opportunity to share the excitement of the World Cup, and for our winners, provide a once-in-a-lifetime experience. We know that if our employees are engaged and motivated, this will positively impact our customers' experience."

The UK McDonald's also used its global sponsorship of the Olympics to run similar incentive programs in the run-up to both the London 2012 and Rio 2016 Summer Olympic Games. When an incentive scheme works, it's well worth repeating!

In Practice

- Use real-life events to create a bit of excitement and variety for your incentive programs or competitions, weaving in branding and experiences to give them more impact.

- Find ways for your incentive programs to target and drive behaviors and actions that make a difference to your business and your customers.

Benefits for the Dogs: *BrewDog*

Situation

It was July 2016, and BrewDog, an independent Scottish brewery and pub chain, had just rolled out its Unicorn Fund, an all-employee profit-sharing plan.[7] According to Allison Green, People Director at BrewDog, "One of the outcomes of the plan was that employees were behaving more like owners, which meant new ideas started rolling in." One of these new ideas came from an employee known only as Squidy, who runs BrewDog's first bar in Scotland. His question was, "For a company so canine-obsessed, why don't we support employees when they get a new dog? They get time off for a new baby, why not a new dog?"

So that's exactly what BrewDog did, introducing a "pawternity" policy, a pooch-based benefit for all staff who get a new dog. And why not? The word "dog" is in the company name, it was founded by two men and a dog, and they have 50 company dogs at their locations around the world.

"Here at BrewDog, we care about many things, but have two main focuses above all others: our beer and our people. But we also just really, really like dogs, so we thought we would combine all three and let our people bring their four-legged friends to work at the brewery and our offices, and take it one step further by offering this latest awesome—or should that be pawesome?—staff perk," says Green.

Play

BrewDog's pawternity benefit, which gives employees one week of fully paid leave, started out as puppy parental leave. However, it's evolved to include anything from a new pup to an unsettled rescue dog—supporting nervy canines and their owners alike, in those all-important first few days of one of the greatest relationships a person can have.

---

[7]More information at rg.co/brewdog

"This benefit has attracted an insane amount of media attention, going absolutely viral. Understandable, since we all love dogs and we all love innovative ideas. But it's important to point out that this wasn't done in isolation; it was part of the bigger picture. We put this benefit in place because it fit in with our company culture and our overall engagement strategy," says Green. It wasn't just a "shiny benefit," as Green calls them, but something that shows employees at BrewDog that they (and their dogs) matter to the business.

What became of Squidy? As recognition for his great idea, the company flew him out to the launch of BrewDog's newest bar in Columbus, Ohio. He already has a pup, so he's not taking any time off, but he did say he's tempted to get a second!

In Practice

- Don't be afraid to create benefits that are a bit different, as long as they align with your company's mission, purpose and values, and aren't done in isolation.

- Not everyone fits the model of a traditional family with children. Look for benefits that go past the normal definition, which can make a significant cultural statement and show that you value diversity.

Creating a Compelling Benefits Communication Campaign: *Citation*

Situation

Citation, an HR legal advice company with an office-based workforce, faced a challenge. The company was rolling out eight new benefits, ranging from a day off for employees' birthdays to wedding and grandparents' leave, to buying and selling days off. How would the team do it in a way that every benefit was both understood and valued? This was an important issue to Linda Jodrell,[8] HR Director. "If you don't message it right, you may as well throw the money down the drain," she says.

The good news was that Citation already had a recognizable benefits brand called "Dave" (which stands for Discounts and Various Exclusives), with a cartoon character of the same name. But how would they make employees realize that Dave had changed with the addition of these new benefits?

They did it by creating an innovative and engaging communications campaign, using a clever teaser approach held together with strong branding. It was highly successful, with 90% of employees engaging with the campaign by registering. It also contributed to a doubling of employee engagement scores, and Citation receiving a classification of "extraordinary" in the UK's *Sunday Times* Top 100 Employers list.

Play

Citation's communication campaign was centered around Dave getting a girlfriend, and was branded as "Introducing Miss Benefit." Jodrell said they created her for a bit of fun, but also to show how Dave was moving into a relationship in the same way that the new benefits were moving into a relationship with the existing ones. Doing this also created a new power couple—one that would increase the overall impact of Citation's communication.

They used a teaser approach to create a sense of excitement, anticipation and interest. On day one, the teaser message was, "After being on his own for the past two years, Dave has decided he would like a lady friend. Before he puts himself out there, he is going to update his image." On the following days, it showed Dave working out, joining a dating site and getting new glasses.

Once properly "teased," employees received gift boxes to bring it all together. Each box contained a document explaining the new benefits, along with chocolates and an invitation to a

---

[8]For a video interview with Linda, visit rg.co/lindajodrell

conference where the company would explain the new benefits. "We wanted to surprise and delight employees, sending the message that the company cared about them," says Jodrell.

In Practice

- Create benefit programs that work together to tell a compelling and connected story.
- Don't be afraid to have some fun with your benefits communications—it can be a great way to grab attention.

Creating a Meaningful Employee Ownership Plan: *Illuminate Education*

Situation

Illuminate Education is the third company Lane Rankin (CEO and President) has started, and he decided that this time around, he was going to do things differently. "I wanted to learn from what I did right and wrong with my previous companies, as well as bring lessons learned from being a teacher, specifically those around engagement," says Rankin.

One lesson or objective was to empower his 200 employees to "create new opportunities for the company while solving problems for our clients," says Rankin. This meant finding ways to create a sense of ownership and empowerment.

To help, Rankin put an employee share plan in place that has shared $60 million with employees over the last eight years. What the company has gotten in return is growing financials, from $150k to more than $34m in seven years, as well as something that Rankin says is their most valued accomplishment: employee loyalty. They've only lost three employees since they started the company, so Rankin must be doing things right.

Play

Illuminate's share plan has created a sense of ownership by making all employees not just shareholders, but *major* shareholders in the company. The profit-sharing plan has rewarded employees handsomely at all levels in the company.

It's paid out a smashing 50% of profits, which is significantly above payouts from most profit-sharing plans, where a higher percentage is saved for the CEO and his or her executives. "It's not about me, Lane, the owner. Rather, it's us in it together," Rankin says. "But you have to put your money where your mouth is." And that's exactly what they did.

In Practice

- Find ways to share the "profits" with your workforce, whether it's financially (such as shares, bonuses) or celebratory (parties). Make your employees feel they're a part of your successes.

- Turn your employees into owners to create a better foundation for discussing profit and business results with everyone.

Turning Tradition on its Head with a Fun Benefits Expo: *3M Australia*

Situation

3M is a company that's normally very traditional, doing things in what could be described as a "corporate way." But with a focus on measuring employee engagement and a desire to make improvements in the area, the Australian Managing Director felt it needed to lighten things up a bit and show the workforce that it was a fun place to work. So, on the heels of introducing two new benefits—a charitable giving program and a leisure and lifestyle benefit—the HR team decided to hold an expo in partnership with their benefit providers at their head office, bringing a bit of fun and, at the same time, helping employees better understand and appreciate their new and existing benefits.

Play

The idea of the expo came from Sebreena Cronin, Talent Development Manager, who frequently takes her young children to school fairs, and thought this format would work well to help lift employee engagement in a fun way. Like a fair, employees were given a ticket to enter the expo, with some even winning a lucky door prize. To create buzz, 3M hired a balloon man who Cronin had seen at a fair, who made elaborate balloon designs. The fun designs enticed employees to want to come and see what all the fun was about, and also helped create conversations throughout the day as they took their balloon masterpieces back to their desks.

The expo consisted of booths run by benefit providers, where employees could stop by and learn more about each benefit. Examples included:

- A booth where employees could learn about discounted movie tickets, and where boxes of popcorn were handed out.
- A booth where employees could learn about discounted bowling experiences, with a mini bowling alley where employees could try and knock down the pins to go into a draw to win a prize.
- A booth where a leasing company answered questions for employees about their individual circumstances, giving away promotional pens, notepads and balloons.
- A booth run by 3M's Corporate Health partner, which offered health checks for employees, held live nutritious cooking demonstrations and ran "healthy food" competitions. Employees could also try out goggles that mimicked

the effect on vision of consuming alcohol to a 0.05 reading, and then trying to "walk the line," represented by tape on the floor.

The expo was a huge success, in fact so much so that the other 11 offices across Australia asked that they be held at their sites. It's too soon to tell how it's affected overall engagement, but it certainly helped raise awareness of the two new benefits as well as existing ones. "The expo was a great way to showcase some wonderful offerings to employees in a very fun way. Seeing smiles all over the office all day due to the experience, which is still talked about today, was certainly a highlight!", says Cronin.

In Practice

- Expos or fairs are a great way to raise awareness and appreciation of your benefit programs. They take a little bit of effort to arrange, but you'll find your benefit providers are more than willing to come and run the booths, and if you have food and games, you won't be able to stop employees from attending.

Improving Collaboration by Removing Sales Commissions: *Bamboo HR*

Situation

Bamboo HR, an organization that creates HR software solutions, had a traditional sales commission plan, based on targets, and paid out when sales were made. That was until Jeff Adams[9] joined the company as CRO, moving from a company that had achieved positive results doing something unconventional: Doing away with sales commissions. Adams had seen first-hand the impact of taking commission off the table, and when he shared this story

---

[9]For a video interview with Jeff, visit rg.co/jeffadams

with the company's founders they were interested to see what it could do for their business and their sales team. And so, in February 2017, Bamboo HR followed suit, and decided to eliminate sales commissions.

It's still early days, but they've seen positive results of this change. "The willingness of sales reps to help each other has improved as the normal friction linked to commissions has gone away. This is important as the company is in hyper growth, so working together and collaborating is critical to be able to keep up with the pace," says Adams.

Play

The team knew that removing sales commissions was a drastic and emotional change, so to ensure its success, they created a comprehensive approach. The first involved determining the "right" salary, something that would be seen as fair and thus motivational for employees. They looked at a variety of factors such as tenure, job level, commissions paid for the previous two years and projected commission for the following year to get the formula right.

Next, the team identified the importance of communicating the change, so instead of rolling out in a group meeting, Adams had one-to-one meetings with each sales rep to explain why this was happening, the new way of thinking and how it would personally affect them. This got all of the questions out of the way so there were no clouds hanging over the change.

And finally, to introduce a way to celebrate hitting individual metrics, the team created a recognition program called "Team on Fire." Leadership worked directly with the sales team to develop the program and align the reward experiences with other experiential rewards awarded at the company.

"We don't believe our salespeople need the extrinsic motivation of a commission plan. They work just as hard now, driven by their intrinsic motivation to do what's right for the business, not having to worry about the complications and confusions created by commission plan design. They collaborate to do what's in the best interest for the business, having more clarity and focus to be able to serve the customer," says Adams.

In Practice

- Question whether your bonus or commission plans are driving employees to meet your business needs and are in line with your culture. If they aren't, change them!
- If you're going to make a big change like this, make sure you create a comprehensive approach to how you design it and how you communicate it—this can be the difference between success and failure.

11

Workspace

Chapter Objectives

In this chapter, we will:

- Understand the evolving role of workspace with employee engagement and productivity.
- Look at ways workspace has to change to meet the needs of the business and our workforces.

Key Points

- Physical and virtual workspaces are enablers and destroyers of employee engagement.
- As jobs become more varied, workspace has taken on a more important and strategic role in employee engagement.
- If our workspaces are to truly "work," we need to take into consideration that work is done in different ways by different people to achieve different objectives.
- Building great workspaces takes courage and a commitment to updating work practices.

Introduction

If I'd written this book two years earlier, this chapter would have been very different. In fact, it might not have been here at all. Workspace wasn't in the early versions of the Bridge™ model; it came as a late, but important, addition to the party.

My initial lack of enthusiasm for this element was caused by my own misunderstanding. First, I thought of it as work*place*, thinking primarily about the physical environment, which invoked thoughts of the lavish workplaces of wealthy companies. I thought they might have a role in recruitment—who doesn't want to work in a cool office?—but I didn't really see the role in longer-term employee engagement.

Things became clearer when I started to understand work*space* as a broader concept: virtual, physical and the wider work environment, including working practices and what we discuss in the next chapter—flexible working. With this new definition and approach, I became convinced that work*space* has an important role as an enabler of engagement and productivity. I'm just as convinced that, unfortunately, many companies still think of it in the context of work*place*, and thus are missing an important engagement tool.

Understanding the Agile Workspace

Where are you based? It's one of the first questions we ask anyone. Even homeworkers are often forced to associate themselves with a base office, as if a connection to one physical corporate space can ensure connection to the people within a company.

With so many companies operating round the clock and around the world, we're beginning to ask ourselves, "Is the connection to a single physical office still important? Or do people need to connect with *people*, who may be anywhere in the world, in any home or office, depending on what projects they are working on at the time?"

Increasingly, we work in cross-departmental teams on projects that form, disband and reform over time, but most of us still tend to sit inflexibly in the same position of the office regardless, glued to a position because we've kept our smelly sneakers in the bottom drawer for years and don't want to empty out all the rubbish!

Sitting Comfortably?

For many of us, our work is more varied than ever before. There are times we need to concentrate and times we need to collaborate, but most of us have to do everything sitting bolt upright in the same chair in the same position at the same desk. If we move to a meeting room, we sit in exactly the same position there.

Today, our offices should provide more options, more alternatives, more different types of seating and—let's be radical—standing! Agile workspace respects the fact that different types of work need different types of space and that, as humans, we actually perform better when we can move around during the day and sit in different places, on different furniture—just like we would naturally at home. Phone calls may be best done from a soundproof calling booth, where you stand up rather than sit. Sofa areas might be better for informal meetings and creative brainstorms. Traditional desks with big screens and their standup cousins might be best for working on spreadsheets or writing a presentation. And homeworking—yes, the fearsome homeworking—might be best for writing a long document or even reading (or writing) a book about employee engagement.

Importantly, agile working is very different from hot-desking, the maligned workplace innovation of the previous decade. **In hot-desking, you lose desks; with agile working, you gain richness of choice and alternatives.**

Hot-desking	Agile working
▪ All the desks are the same.	▪ There are many different types of working areas for tasks like reading, writing, calling, presenting, collaborating or meeting.
▪ There are fewer desks than people.	
▪ There is perceived competition for resources.	▪ There are more places to work than people, but fewer traditional desks than people.
▪ There is no advantage over a permanent desk.	▪ People feel they have gained something.
▪ People feel they have lost something.	

Modern agile workspaces feel much more like cafés or hotel lobbies. They are designed to maximize unexpected collisions and unplanned conversations between people. When Steve Jobs was CEO of Pixar, he famously tried to have only one set of bathrooms, deliberately trying to create a bottleneck where people could meet. In the end, they settled on a central atrium.

"The best workplaces combine spaces, services, and culture to create a great experience for employees and customers."
—Elliot Felix, Founder at Brightspot Strategy

Whether it's through planned collisions in spaces such as meeting rooms or casual collisions in other shared spaces, these interactions are all valuable for collaboration.

Technology's Role to Play

Technology has an increasing role to play in how we experience the office—it's the systems and products you use as much as the desks and chairs and sofas. But at work, many of our systems are antiquated: old and clunky. Some still use mainframe apps designed in the 1970s. That's why 72% of our employees say they struggle to find information they need easily, making technology a significant source of work related stress.

When we think about the role of workspace, we need to think about the whole workspace: the hardware *and* the software. It's no good having a great office if the technology on the desks is hard to use, frustrating or obsolete. All the good work you can do on the Bridge™ will be undermined if the basic tools you give your staff don't help them do their best work.

Embracing the cloud and modern communications systems like Slack, Yammer or Workplace by Facebook is key. These can feel scary, since their key role is to open up and democratize information, making it easier to search and find and harder to hide, but you'll soon wonder how you lived without them.

In Practice

When we think about workspace, we need to think about how the space we work in—both physical and virtual—makes our people feel. Does it make them feel proud? Engaged? Excited? Or frustrated?

> "*Companies need to create spaces where form and function create a workplace experience that tells your story, involves users and delights visitors.*"
> —Andrea Williams-Wedberg, Agile Workspace Designer

Key Benefits

There are several key benefits to an effective workspace.

Increased Productivity A well-designed workspace can have a meaningful and lasting impact on the productivity of your workforce. Whether it's in the physical workspace, designing space for both collaboration and reflection, or having the right technology, if done properly, the right design can maximize your workforce's potential, performance and productivity.

Improved Talent Attraction I once heard someone refer to the workspace as the new company car—a tool for attracting talent to our organizations. The workspace is often the first impression for a candidate, so it can be a powerful magnet or detractor in their decision to join your company.

Increased Collaboration Developing a company's workspace to create formal or informal "collisions" can have a profound impact on collaboration. Creating space and putting tools in place to help build relationships between people and between teams helps your people work together more often and in more effective ways.

Ability to Bring Your Whole Self to Work By designing your workspace to meet the needs of your diverse workforce, you can provide the opportunity to "bring your whole self to work." This not only creates success and satisfaction in ourselves, but has the biggest impact on our abilities to get the work done.

Key Rebel Behaviors

In companies that get workspace right, rebels act in these ways.

1. **Collaborate with courage**
   Rebels collaborate with their workforces to understand their needs and communicate with them often. But they do this

with courage—many people are highly resistant to change, especially in terms of physical workspace, but rebels balance collaboration with the courage to take a bold step into the future. You *can* build a paperless office and you *can* move to true agile working, but don't expect everyone to be excited about the move in advance.

2. **Make room for differences**
   Rebels understand that there is no "one-size-fits-all" approach to workspaces. They build in room for differences, allowing their employees to be true to themselves in how and when they work.

3. **Are brave**
   Rebels know they may have to try new and different things to get their workspaces right, and aren't afraid to try them. However, they understand the importance of being strategic when it comes to bravery, not thinking the latest and greatest workspace gimmick will help them achieve their goals.

4. **Make values prominent**
   Rebels know that their values have to be front and center in the design of their workspaces, because if not, they know they're missing an important trick. Values should ooze off the walls, with employees reminded of them as they go about their work.

5. **Constantly iterate**
   Rebels know that their job is never done when it comes to their workspaces. They are constantly checking in with the business and their workforces to ensure that a space continues to meet their needs and delivers on their objectives.

Making a Start

Employees themselves instinctively know what works for most parts of the Bridge™—they can teach us a lot about what is needed in leadership, communication and recognition. But that's not universally true with workspace. There is something special about the human condition that connects us to the status quo where physical workspace is concerned, making us resistant to change even when we're in the worst of conditions.

I remember when Reward Gateway was in its old London office, which was falling apart after years of near-zero investment. I walked through the finance department and saw one of our assistants, Tina, wearing three layers of clothes, a scarf and a hat. She was sitting directly under an air-conditioning vent that was blasting out cold air. When I suggested she move to any of the three empty desks close by, she looked at me in shock. "No, I like it here, this is my desk!"

People dislike physical workspace change more than any other aspect of work that I know, so when it comes to workspace, you'll need to let your inner rebel out. Making change will require courage.

Assess Your Workspace Requirements   Start by looking at the work that has to be done and the workspace requirements associated with it. Do you have the right amount of quiet space? Collaboration space? Is it actually comfortable? Map out what work has to be done, and compare this to the spaces that currently exist. From there, you can assess whether you need to make any changes that would make your workspace more engaged and productive.

Get Employee Input and Feedback   Before making significant workspace changes, it's important to have your employees provide input and feedback. Hold focus groups to discuss how they work currently and what needs to be done in the future to make them more effective. Working with the model of agile working, what can be changed in your current workspace to make it a better environment for your workforce?

Be Inspired   Lots of great workspaces have gotten it right, so go out there and get inspiration from them. Give them a call and visit them, read about them, or check out **rg.co/ inspiredworkspaces** for some videos and online inspiration.

THE PLAYS

Creating a Workspace to Drive Agile Working: *GE*

Situation

GE had what you'd call traditional offices. Like many large organizations, job grades drove the size of the office, right down to the number of square meters. However, when a new CEO joined the business in 2014, he challenged the business to move to the concept of "agile working," which is all about creating different work areas within the office, giving employees freedom and flexibility to work where they want, when they want.

When GE's office in Sydney, Australia, moved to this new approach, there was a sense of fear and some resistance at the beginning, says David Arkell, HR Leader Australia. To overcome this, the original plan was to create a phased approach, doing one floor at a time, taking three years to complete the entire fit-out. However, according to Arkell, "Once the first three groups went into the workspace, they loved it so much that everyone else wanted to give it a go. It's created a new way of working. Before we were very siloed, but now employees from different groups sit next to each other, creating an environment of sharing and collaboration."

Play

GE's new workspace is designed not only as an agile workplace, but one that uses the concept of "activity-based working." This recognizes that employees engage in a variety of different work and activities throughout the day, having different physical requirements. In the new office, the only permanent thing is the employee's home-floor locker, with everything else being temporary and fluid, and employees moving throughout the building to the space that is most effective for the work they're carrying out at a given moment. It's so fluid that in locations where there are two offices, employees are even given the choice of which office they want to go to. "We don't care where they work; it's the output and not the input that is important to us," says Arkell.

The survey, conducted before and after the changes, found employees were significantly more satisfied with their workspace, felt it promoted a culture of innovation, and favored GE as an Employer of Choice. It's also aligned with two words that are used regularly—"choice" and "inclusivity." "By giving our people the choice to choose where and when they work, we are helping them bring their actual selves to work and realize their true potential," says Arkell. It's been such a success that other GE offices have adopted this approach to workspace design.

In Practice

- Review your workspace to ensure it supports your people as they carry out their different work and activities throughout the day. If it doesn't, then look for ways to make changes to support the concept of "activity-based working."

A Workspace Where You Want to Bring Your Mom: *Pentland Brands*

Situation

Pentland's head office in London was at capacity—not enough room for its growing workforce, and no room to display and archive its wide range of sports, outdoor and fashion products. Andy Rubin, chairman of this family-owned business, set out to create a new workspace, one where employees wanted to come to work, where products could be designed better and sum up all of the company's many brands.

Rubin brought in the company's Creative Director, Katie Greenyer,[1] who set out to design a workspace that "has a soul and character, is inspiring, and is a place where you want to bring your mum." She used her vision and experience as a fashion designer to develop the office, contributing to Pentland winning the British Council of Offices award for its design. The accolades didn't stop there: The new design earned a spot in Great Places to Work's "Best Workplaces" list, and engagement survey results said that 93% were proud to tell others they worked for Pentland, 85% that people care about each other and 83% that it was a fun place to work.

Play

When you see the Pentland office, it's no surprise that employees responded as they did in the engagement survey. The space speaks of caring for employees, with onsite facilities any company would be proud of (subsidized restaurant, tennis courts, full-purpose gym, pool tables, indoor pool, etc.), as well as areas that encourage community, such as the canteen featuring benches instead of chairs. Family and community is ever-present, especially down a hallway that tells the company's history through pictures and historical documents mounted on the wall.

Greenyer encouraged the team to be innovative in all aspects of the design, including room names. Naming the rooms based on electricity was a nod to the former use of the office as a power station. "This created a design hook, telling a story and creating interest and engagement," she says. To add to the innovation, the company held a competition with university students to design what Greenyer calls "things you can't buy off the shelf," such as furniture, ceramics, sculpture, art and rugs. This not only opened doors for future designers; it produced unique

---

[1]For a video interview with Katie, visit rg.co/katiegreenyer

designs for the office. It was also the start of "Design Pool," which has become an ongoing apprenticeship program for university students.

All in all, the office achieved its objective of being a place where collaboration happens to support designing better products, and where employees want to come to work, and yes, perhaps even bring their mothers!

In Practice

- Find ways to bring your company's history into your workspace. It can be a powerful reminder of who you are and how you got to where you are.

- Get creative when it comes to finding people to help design your office. Consider whether there are others, either within or outside your company, who can add interesting perspectives.

Designing a Workspace Using All of Your Senses: *Adobe*

Situation

Adobe is a company that creates multimedia visual products, so it should be no surprise that its offices are stunning, with each being a visual delight. But is that enough? According to Eric Kline,[2] Director of Global Workplace Design at Adobe, the answer is no. Adobe believes its workspaces "need to create and amplify culture through all of the amazing experiences that bring people together and allow them to be their best self," says Kline.

With this goal, the Adobe team set off to create offices that are more than just spaces–they are spaces that engage and speak

---

[2]For a video interview with Eric, visit rg.co/erickline

to their employees. They've done this by using design techniques that take into account all of our senses and reflect all of our differences. "Because people are so different in how they live and how they work, we wanted to make sure that not one sense or one type dominated the design, but that they are all taken into account and layered into the experience" says Kline.

Adobe offices have not only won awards for the design, but it's contributed to the company landing coveted spots on *Fortune*'s "100 Best Companies to Work For" and Glassdoor's "Best Places to Work" lists.

Play

Adobe's offices have been designed to stimulate each of the five senses to deliver the greatest impact and experience for the workforce. Each sense has been considered, individually and collectively, to transform Adobe offices into spaces that evoke emotion and increase engagement and productivity at many levels. Colors have been used to influence behavior and create energy. Sustainable natural materials such as wood and plants have been used to bring the calming effects of nature into the office and, at the same time, show respect for the environment. Scents have been used to help employees feel calm, invigorated or welcomed. Even music has been used thoughtfully to drive comfort levels and enhance conversations.

An example is the newly renovated auditorium at their San Jose, California, headquarters. It previously had a corporate feel with marble floors and walls, artificial plants and a sterile staircase, which was less a reflection of the Adobe brand. "It could have been any company," says Kline. The team completely transformed the space, bringing in colors and textures, as well as immersive environmental branding, to make it look and feel like an Adobe space and experience.

Another example is a conference room wall, which, at first glance, looks like an ordinary wall with plastic plants hanging on it. However, if you look closer (and touch or smell), you'll notice that the wall is actually covered in living plants. To appeal to even more senses and create a greater experience, edible plants were hung in their place for the holiday party.

These, and many more examples, illustrate how Adobe has used workspace design and the five senses to create experiences. As Kline says, "Each experience creates an opportunity. What if two employees, drawn together because of the aroma of fresh-baked cookies, come together to create the company's next great idea? We try to find unique yet natural ways to bring our people and innovation together."

In Practice

- Find ways to bring each of your senses into your workspace. Making even little changes and adding small touches can make a difference in creating a better experience for your workforce.

- Find ways to make your office more than just a space, creating experiences to appeal to your entire workforce.

A Workspace Fit for Kings and Queens: *money.co.uk*

Situation

When Chris Morling, Managing Director of money.co.uk, a financial comparison website, set out to refurbish the company's office in the Cotswolds, he faced both a challenge and a responsibility—a challenge in that the building was a Grade II listed castle, meaning there were strict guidelines on what can be done, and a responsibility, both to the space and to the workforce.

"Looking after your team is paramount. Your team is your engine, so it's really important you look after them and give them the best of everything. That stretches from how we work, to benefits, right through to the actual working environment. If you get that right, you have a strong, motivated team to drive you forward. You spend half your working life in the office, and I wanted to create a motivating, uplifting environment that gave them flexibility and encouraged collaboration," says Morling.

Knowing they wanted to respect the grandeur and heritage of the castle and, at the same time, make it a bit fun and wacky to reflect the personality of the company, Morling brought in Laurence Llewelyn-Bowen, a homestyle consultant and TV presenter who's known for being far from traditional.

"Something big and bouncy and brave had to happen to an unusual building; it needed someone like Chris to not feel it should be understated. There are lots of faddish, whimsical, patronizing designs that happen to offices, which I wanted to avoid. I wanted to make sure the relationship of my designs worked with the culture of the company, and the style and age of the building itself," says Llewelyn-Bowen.

The result is the creation of a workspace that's "significantly changed how we work, making a massive difference in how we collaborate and how we have fun," says Morling.

Play

The first phase of the project focused on functionality, with the aim of opening up and redesigning the space to support collaboration. Employees were brought together to ask what they wanted and needed to make their work both easier and more enjoyable. Their feedback led to the design of collaboration space, as well as space for quiet work and reflection, and—of course—fun. Every detail has been thought through, from the large screen to communicate to the entire workforce, to furniture that's 100% flexible to move, to the workspace for wellness activities.

The second phase involved weaving the company's personality into the office, putting its own stamp on the design. This is shown in spaces such as a Star Wars cinema room, steampunk toilets playing classical music, an ice cave and a ski lodge, all showing the fun personality of the company.

The new office sends the message loud and clear to employees, customers and prospective employees: That money.co.uk cares about its people. By doing things in a way that combines functionality and fun, the company has created an award-winning space for their "kings and queens" to work and play.

In Practice

- It's important to design workspaces to support and drive functionality, not just fun. This ensures that it's not just a pretty place to work, but one that will drive results on an ongoing basis.

- Don't be afraid to bring your company's personality to your office design; it shows and reminds your employees and customers who you are and what you stand for.

12

Wellbeing

Chapter Objectives

In this chapter, we will:

- Discuss how to create an integrated approach to wellbeing.
- Explain how workplace stress and burnout is the key threat to business performance.
- Look at the importance of moving away from a one-sided approach to true flexible working.

Key Points

- Wellbeing needs an integrated approach covering physical, financial and mental health to be effective.
- Technology has fundamentally changed the relationship between home and work, and our mishandling of that has led to record stress levels.
- Flexible working in its current state is not flexible.
- Tackling the root causes of wellbeing issues will require complete buy-in from your entire organization.

Introduction

I've been working in and around employee wellbeing for nearly 25 years and in that time, the collective thinking about wellbeing has moved on hugely. Back in the 1990s, we focused almost entirely on a reactive approach to wellbeing with the aim of reducing absence days and, in the US at least, trying to get a grip on the burgeoning cost of healthcare. Now, the most progressive companies are lining up to an integrated and proactive approach for tackling the biggest demons of workplace wellbeing.

Wellbeing is No Longer a "Nice To Do" For Companies; It is a "Have To Do"

It's no longer giving out free gym memberships or free fruit; it's addressing and tackling wellbeing in an integrated way. Stick with the old ways and you'll have employees who exercise and like fruit, but are still stressed and burnt out like all the rest.

We Need More Than Free Bananas

If you needed a "silver bullet" for getting wellbeing right, it would be to create a fully integrated approach. Do this and you're well on your way to reaping the benefits: significantly reducing absenteeism, increasing employee engagement and improving resilience to stress—three things any business needs to succeed.

To achieve this, your approach needs three key strands:

Physical

Helping employees with healthier eating and activity

1 in 4 are not active enough

Physical inactivity is the 4th leading cause of global mortality

Mental

Helping employees with stress, depression + mental illness

1 in 4 experience a mental health problem yearly

Financial

Helping employees with debt, overspending + money management

53% are stressed about finance + 50% have difficulty making minimum credit card payments[1]

Physical wellbeing is the area most commonly addressed, but that's because it's where most companies and wellbeing products began, as well as the most visible area of concern. The most successful of these programs combine improved access, for example, by discounted or subsidized gym memberships, with continuous education and information about how to improve activity.

The other two areas—mental and financial—are arguably even more important, but are often ignored or avoided because there is an understandable fear or taboo associated with them. But the truth is that financial wellbeing, or the lack of it, has a terrible impact on the concentration and capability of your staff, leading to a domino effect of wider mental wellbeing issues causing reduced performance.

---

[1]For more information on wellbeing pillars, visit rg.co/wellbeingpillar

> ## We Need Our People to Do More than Show Up These Days
>
> The demands we make on people are so much more than they used to be. We used to need people to show up and turn the handle on the machine. Now we want them to show up and be creative, innovate, make great decisions, have amazing ideas and deliver great service—we need so much more from them. They can't do all that if they're worried sick about money, stressed, depressed or exhausted.

Our Stress and Burnout Crisis

The watershed moment in my personal relationship with wellbeing was a talk by Arianna Huffington at a conference in 2013. Commenting on a moving op-ed piece[2] in the *New York Times* where ex-Lehman Brothers CFO Erin Callan talked about how she'd had no life after devoting herself to work for 20 years, Arianna pointed out, "...and Lehman still went bankrupt":

> *"That's the thing I want everybody to understand. It's not like it's a trade-off, like 'I'm just going to build this great company, and the hell with my relationships and my life and my health.' No, you can no longer do that. The world is moving so fast, change is happening at such overwhelming speed, that if you are not really connected with your own wisdom, your own intuition ..."*[3]

That's such a critical point: We can't have it all. Technology is fueling disruption from all sides and we need skill, judgment and higher-level thinking from more of our employees than ever

---

[2] *New York Times* article at **rg.co/erincallan**.
[3] Video and full text at **rg.co/arianna**.

before, but judgment and creativity suffer when we're exhausted. That's what makes chronic workplace stress such an effective destroyer of company performance.

Wellbeing Isn't a Benefit Any More— It's a Key People Strategy

We used to "do wellbeing" to be nice to the individual. Work-life balance was about the person. Now we need our people to come to work, have great judgment and "see the icebergs before they hit the *Titanic*," but they can't do that if they are exhausted and burnt out. Now we need to "do wellbeing" because it's absolutely essential for the organization.

The problem is we're working more hours than ever, but with no measurable impact on productivity because the extra hours just aren't productive. Along with more hours, we're also working with greater intensity than ever. Always-on technology is bombarding us with constant messages, e-mails, texts, tweets 24/7, creating an "always available" expectation. For many of us, our performance is more measurable, visible and tracked than ever before. We are exposed and under pressure, dealing with tougher competition and constantly being asked for, and communicating, our results. Deloitte's Human Capital Trends report uses a term, "*the overwhelmed employee*," to describe the multitude of roles and competing demands for our time that we have today.

It seems, though, that there's a limit on what is humanly possible for most of us. The 2016 GCC Insights report found that while the average worker took four days off sick each year, they admitted to being too tired or stressed to be fully productive on a staggering 57 days per year.[4] That equates to $1.5 trillion per year in lost work. GCC's Chief Medical Officer, Dr. David Batman, said, "We need to stop talking about how many sick days

---

[4] rg.co/gccinsights2016

people are taking and focus our energy on what they're doing when they're actually at work."[5]

The Smoking Gun is Our One-sided Relationship with Flexible Working

Technology has made the lines between work and home impossibly blurred, but many corporations behave as if nothing has changed. When I asked a friend of mine, an architect, if his practice offered flexible working, he said, "Sure: We can do what we want, as long as we're at our desks for core hours of 9.15 a.m. to 6 p.m." I thought he was being sarcastic, but he thought this was OK.

Whilst most companies pay lip-service to flexible working, requiring people to ask permission to work flexibly, the truth is that they don't like mutual flexibility. Companies embraced self-serving, one-sided flexibility decades ago when they encouraged us to access e-mail remotely. Work encroached on the sanctity of home, but most companies have been stubborn about allowing home life into the office.

Inflexible Working Creates Unnecessary, Unproductive Stress

Productive stress is the natural tension that exists to get things done.

Unproductive stress is tension caused by complying with unrelated rules that don't help get the job done. Unproductive stresses create no value for the business; they are pointless and even destructive, and make it less likely, not more, that you will achieve your goals. Business is full of unproductive stress!

---

[5]http://www.ehstoday.com/safety-leadership/presenteeism-costs-business-10-times-more-absenteeism.

If we want flexible working to work, we need to shift the power. We have to change our default response from *no* to *yes*. Rather than ask employees to bravely beg for different hours, we have to invert the process and make managers write a business case to prevent someone from working flexibly. Flexible working has to stop being a privilege and be an expectation—and yes, that means we should remove it from our list of company benefits, too.

When a manager writes that they just don't trust someone, we need to ask what they're doing about that—if we can't trust someone with something as simple as choosing their location and hours for a particular day, how can we trust them to manage our clients, design our products or run our accounts?

Companies can no longer hide behind a one-sided approach to flexible working. It doesn't work—not for the company and not for the workforce. They need to move to a mutual, two-sided approach. Failure to provide equitable flexibility in return creates a culture of "presenteeism" and overwork.

Finally, for a two-sided flexible working approach to work, it absolutely must have strong and visible leadership by example, from the top down and throughout the business. Without this, like every other section of the Bridge™, it will fail.

How does that work? For years, I've put every haircut and daily gym workout in my calendar for everyone to see, which helps to normalize flexible working as something everyone can do as routine.

In Practice

Key Outcomes Rebels Strive For

Lower Sickness Absence and Stress Leave   In the US alone, a million workers miss work every single day due to stress, with a further $1.5 trillion in estimated lost productivity from staff coming to work stressed and unable to perform to the fullest.

Rebels strive to reduce this, focusing on the quality of work and results more than the quantity, valuing productivity over presenteeism.

Better Creativity and Innovation   Stressed-out staff create and innovate less because they're investing their energy in just getting through the day. By removing these obstacles, you make them free to come up with the next great ideas for your company.

Improved Decision-Making   Rebels who successfully manage wellbeing benefit from significantly better decisions. Employees are sharper and more focused, thus able to create better solutions for the business and its customers.

Key Rebel Behaviors

Out of everything on the Bridge™, the wellbeing element as a profession is perhaps the least developed, although we still see some evolving consistencies amongst high-performing rebels.

1. **Embed flexible working deeply**
   Rebels avoid permission-based flexible working and evolve a culture of complete trust where there is mutual, two-way flexibility. They popularize the notion that *inflexible working* is a route to burnout and is counter-cultural.
2. **Tackle the hard issues**
   Rebels understand both the challenges and sensitivities of wellbeing initiatives, and aren't afraid to go after them head on. They focus on the positive outcomes and influence business leaders to take the necessary steps for their wellbeing journeys. They don't just go after those already engaged with wellbeing, but actively go after the disengaged.
3. **Provide a personalized approach**
   Rebels understand that there is no "one-size-fits-all" solution when it comes to wellbeing; it has to be unique to each person.

They support a range of interventions and provide varied help, allowing employees to make their own choices based on their own personal priorities.

4. **Embed deeply in the culture**
   Rebels know that an effective wellbeing program is not about one-off initiatives that only engage a small percentage of an organization. They create a culture of wellbeing that is at the core of how their organization fulfills its mission, and is lived and breathed by all employees every day through its operations and values.

5. **Remove the friction**
   Rebels often find ways to reduce the friction or challenges associated with wellbeing, either financially or from a convenience perspective. This could mean subsidizing healthy canteen choices, discounted gym memberships or onsite mindfulness classes. They remove obstacles that come between their employees and wellbeing, supporting them in achieving their individual goals.

Making a Start

Make a Commitment   The only way for companies to change the deeply concerning wellbeing statistics is to commit to making wellbeing a priority. Set a clear wellbeing strategy at your company, get your leadership team on board, and do whatever it takes to ensure that wellbeing—and I mean an integrated approach to wellbeing—is clearly and firmly on your organization's agenda.

Assess the Needs of Your Workforce   Go out there and learn the wellbeing needs of your workforce, assessing what programs and support are required to make a difference in their work and personal lives. Use this to help set the direction and course of your wellbeing journey, constantly monitoring it to ensure you are continually on track.

Change How You Work   If you truly want to make a difference in the health of your workforce, and thus the health of your
organization, you have to fundamentally take a step back and
look at how you work. What policies and practices do you have
in place that are preventing employees from achieving their wellbeing goals, from having two-way flexible working arrangements
to dealing with stress? Change or remove those that are obstacles, and give your workforce the opportunity to make wellbeing
a priority.

THE PLAYS

Creating Flexibility to Support Diversity: *Boston Consulting Group*

Situation

Management consultants at the Boston Consulting Group (BCG)
faced a challenge common to many in the professional services
industry: that of the "always on" mentality. With a team of consultants driven to support clients, how could the company support its own clients—the employees? With the strain and stress
of the job, and its impact on personal life being the top reason
employees were leaving, what could they do to help retain these
important and valuable assets?

   The solution was to find a "better way to work," identifying
different ways to manage how work gets done to help consultants sustain longer, more satisfying careers. "Often companies
put in place cosmetic work–life balance programs, ones that
address the outer layer of the problem such as letting employees
work from home, but they don't address the core problem. At
BCG, we wanted to go to the core and address changing the
nature of work, finding different ways to manage downtime,"
says Meldon Wolfgang, Senior Partner and Managing Director.

Teaming up with Professor Leslie Perlow of the Harvard Business School, BCG conducted experiments with this concept, which led to creating a program called "PTO". "Our experiments with time off resulted in more open dialogue among team members, which is valuable in itself, but the improved communication also sparked new processes that enhanced the team's ability to work most efficiently and effectively," says Perlow.

Play

The PTO experiment was such a success that it's become a way of working globally at BCG and used for all consulting projects. The model has three parts.

P—predictability, which is about adding a sense of order and visibility to the work. "By removing the feeling of being out of control, you're removing the stress that can drain employees of energy," says Wolfgang. One way of doing this is for employees to protect a set time—typically one night each week—that forces active team discussions about prioritization and focuses on the highest-value efforts.

T—Predictability only happens if you have a team that works together effectively, which involves **teaming**. Teams are supported by experienced facilitators responsible for leading a regular open forum for sharing team progress and needs, whether it's urgent work or taking time off to spend with family or friends. The result is an environment to discuss how and when work gets done.

O—This wouldn't happen without the last element of the model, **open communication**. When teams have open and honest dialogues, they collectively challenge work and assumptions, enabling them to achieve business and personal goals.

This new way of working has had many positive effects at BCG: 74% of consultants say they're more likely to stay with BCG, teamwork and collaboration have increased by 35%, the value delivered to clients has increased by 35%, and—last but not least—BCG rose to number three on *Fortune*'s "100 Best Companies to Work For" list in 2017. As one consultant noted, "PTO has removed the historical industry stigma around admitting 'I am stressed.' We have very candid and actionable conversations during our biweekly PTO checkpoints, where we talk about how we're 'really feeling' and what we can tangibly do to make it better. As a result, a challenging job feels incredibly manageable."

In Practice

- This model shows that change is possible when it's owned collectively. Build a mechanism and approach to take collective ownership of the way teams work from the start.
- Recognize that unpredictability can and will cause problems, and find ways to remove this so your employees can take back their lives.

A Holistic Approach to Financial Wellbeing: *Travis Perkins PLC*

Situation

Travis Perkins PLC, the UK's largest supplier of building materials, decided to focus its attention on the financial wellbeing of its more than 24,000 employees. According to Paul Nelson, Group Head of Reward, "Financial challenges for many of our colleagues are the most serious issue they are grappling with today. It is inevitable that those issues come into work with them and affect how they go about their jobs and how they interact with our customers."

The company set out to develop a financial wellbeing program to improve the overall wellbeing of the workforce and the organization. It began by creating a comprehensive set of objectives focused on improving employee engagement, reducing absence, improving safety, embracing the multigenerational workforce and being seen as an employer of choice.

The program had to be multifaceted to achieve all of these objectives. "We wanted to build a mature, modern, comprehensive financial wellbeing strategy, from saving to investing and knowledge and education to intervention and support," says Carol Kavanagh, Group HR Director. The award-winning program definitely ticked these boxes, and will continue to do so as they make further progress and improvements in the financial health and wellbeing of colleagues.

Play

Travis Perkins created a unique and comprehensive suite of solutions aimed at meeting the needs of a diverse workforce. They did this by looking at and addressing financial wellbeing in two key ways.

First, they mapped out what they called an employee's "life journey," looking at the financial situations that employees faced at different stages of their lives—from when they begin their careers all the way out to retirement. Some points on the typical journey included dealing with student loans, buying a first home, getting married, having children and caring for dependents.

Next, they mapped out an employee's "financial health," creating three health categories, from slipping to balanced and, finally, to comfortable.

With these two areas clearly mapped out, they next aligned the products and programs they'd put in place to improve the financial health of all employees, regardless of life stage. They used strategic partners to deliver financial products, awareness and education relevant and unique to each life stage and challenge.

This end-to-end approach was key, because "people need life skills on how to manage their finances. There's little point having financial products if they don't have enough information to decide how to pick and choose them," says Simon Naylor, Head of Group Benefits. This holistic approach is paying off, and now Travis Perkins is looking at how to build out the next stage of the journey with the introduction of savings-led products, so that once colleagues achieve balance, they are "nudged" to consider how they can start saving for comfortable futures.

In Practice

- When developing a financial wellbeing program, see things through the eyes of your workforce. Understand their situations and needs upfront, and use these to create the backbone of your program.

- Be brave. It can be scary to involve yourself in the personal finances of your employees, but debt and credit management is a real issue for many staff that can be hugely distracting from work, so don't be afraid to find ways to support them.

Using Leaders to Champion Wellbeing: *American Express*

Situation

American Express decided it wanted to create a long-term approach to wellbeing for its 55,000 employees in 35 countries. According to Breckon Jones, Director, Total Reward, "We wanted to transform our culture and what we value, putting wellbeing front and center, making it a global priority." The company began a phased approach, with phase one being the development of *Healthy Living*, an innovative global wellbeing program and brand platform. "We always had a great range of health benefits that employees could leverage across our operating markets," says Jones. "However, these benefits were not linked, resulting in a disconnected employee experience. Much of this phase was focused on repackaging our employee communications: highlighting the full spectrum of benefits at their fingertips."

The program has been a huge success, winning numerous awards. More importantly, it's helped the company achieve its objectives to increase physical activity while helping reduce the negative effects of stress and obesity.

To continue embedding wellbeing into the DNA of the organization, American Express decided that phase two would involve focusing on creating champions for the program and the health of individual teams.

Play

The aim of phase two was to identify ways to help middle managers understand the benefits of good health and its impact on employee engagement, while engaging them as champions of the Healthy Living program. "You need to ensure leaders understand the personal benefits of the program to them and their direct reports. It's then that you can capture their attention and encourage leaders to become more invested in the health of their teams and enable them to identify potential health issues," says Jones.

American Express did this in a few ways. First, the company added wellbeing questions to the employee engagement survey, giving the organization and leaders a baseline of information to better understand and monitor the wellbeing of their teams. Second, it built wellbeing education modules just for leaders into the company's learning platform, to help them understand both the strategy and details of the program. Last, it created a global site accreditation program, with leaders answering a questionnaire about ways they're bringing Healthy Living to life for their employees and receiving plaques to celebrate their sites' accreditation. "Many have become true champions, driving further changes in wellbeing," says Jones.

Today, 96% of American Express employees globally have access to at least one wellbeing initiative, including 24 onsite clinics and wellbeing centers in offices in 12 markets.

In Practice

- It's important to engage your leaders if you want your wellbeing program to be successful. If they believe and support it, you've got that many more voices out there talking about and driving it.

- Find ways to introduce learning modules to ensure your leaders get the support they need to be true champions.

A Way to "PerkUp" Your Wellbeing Benefit: *LinkedIn*

Situation

Many companies put innovative and occasionally bizarre perks in place, using these to stand out and differentiate themselves in the war for talent. LinkedIn, a company that has won awards such as Glassdoor's "Best Places to Work" and *Forbes'* "America's Best Employers," decided they wanted to look at perks differently.

They decided to create "perks with a purpose," according to Nina McQueen,[6] VP Global Benefits & Employee Experience. Says McQueen, "Everything we do in benefits must serve a purpose: whether for the business or because it's simply the right thing to do. The last thing we want is to put in benefit programs that are really just building a house of cards. We would like for our programs to have staying power. We want our programs to make a difference in people's lives."

LinkedIn set out to design a wellbeing perk that would do just that: Make an impact and difference in the lives of their employees. They looked externally, participating in a newly created "values of perks" survey in Silicon Valley (the home of wild perks), and surveying employees internally, asking "What

---

[6]For a video interview with Nina, visit rg.co/ninamcqueen.

would make a difference to you?" The result was a highly unique and personalized approach to perks, a program called *PerkUp!*

Play

The PerkUp! benefit gives employees an annual allowance that varies by country (it's $2,000/year in the US). It can be used to spend on perks from an approved list, including gym memberships, personal trainers, fitness classes, massages, childcare, pet-sitting and dog-walking. "It focuses on perks that improve employee wellbeing or create convenience to make employees' lives easier," says McQueen.

The program gives employees the opportunity and flexibility to choose perks that best fit their needs, personalizing it to them. Eligible categories were originally based on what employees indicated mattered most to them via survey feedback, and then fine-tuned after a three-month global pilot.

PerkUp! has been a huge success, with 80% of employees globally using the benefit. It's been a win–win for the company and employees, giving the company a benefit that *shows employees they care*, and providing a *competitive advantage* (recruiters have said it is a "wow" factor when talking to candidates), and giving employees something *they've asked for* and *have control over*. It's definitely "perked things up" at LinkedIn by delivering a benefit with purpose and meaning.

In Practice

- If you can't find data you need, consider hosting or sponsoring a survey. You'll be surprised that you're not the only person wanting this information.

- When developing a wellbeing benefit, find ways to build meaning and purpose into it, offering elements that stand out and have the "wow" factor.

Taking Small But Meaningful Steps to Wellbeing: *GreatCall*

Situation

GreatCall is a company providing health and safety products and services to older adults and caregivers. From a people perspective, this means having a workforce that's not only engaged, but healthy enough to meet the needs of their customers, who rely on them 24/7.

With a health-focused culture, but having no budget and no physical space for wellbeing activities, Lynn Herrick, Chief HR Officer, knew she had a challenge. However, inspired by a Gloria Steinem talk about how small changes can make a big impact, Herrick set out to begin the company's wellbeing journey by making small but powerful steps, proving the importance of taking that first step if you want to make a difference.

Play

The first step for GreatCall's wellbeing program was offering free on-site yoga classes. Sounds easy—but it isn't if you don't have space. That didn't stop them; they just did yoga in between cubicles. This sent a clear message to employees that the company wanted to make wellbeing accessible by bringing it into the workplace.

According to Herrick, "If you want to show your employees that you're serious about supporting their wellbeing, you need to find ways to bring it into the workplace. We believe that many wouldn't have had the time or commitment if they had to do it outside working hours."

The next steps involved adding other exercise classes, as well as a wide range of initiatives focusing on mental health and financial wellbeing. Complementing these was the introduction of "meaningful days," aligning with GreatCall's mission statement: "meaningful work and living a meaningful life." These days allowed employees to take one paid day off each month to do something personally meaningful to them, thus defining wellbeing in their own ways.

These small steps added up to a comprehensive and successful wellbeing program that received fantastic employee feedback and positive business results. Since the program has been in place, GreatCall has enjoyed a a more collaborative working environment, breaking down barriers as employees from all areas exercise side by side. According to CEO David Inns, the program creates a "culture of motivation," with employees at all levels being motivated to get out from behind their desks and interact with each other on a personal level. According to Herrick, it's also made recruitment easier, has reduced turnover and given the company its most successful three years since the program has been in place.

In Practice

- Don't let challenges or barriers prevent you from creating wellbeing programs. You can overcome those by taking small but meaningful steps.
- Create an overall wellbeing plan, ensuring that the steps you take lead up to your overall objectives.

A Benefit to Help Fight Employee Burnout: *Weebly*

Situation

Weebly, a web-hosting service, has the challenge that many technology companies face in Silicon Valley: To win the war for talent.

With this aim in mind, they decided to create a benefit that would help them stand out from the pack, creating something as unique as the websites their services allow their clients to create, and one that would truly make a difference for employees and the business.

Play

The new benefit Weebly introduced was a sabbatical program offered to employees with five or more years of service. Employees, or "Weeblies" as they're called, receive six weeks paid time off as well as free roundtrip airfare to anywhere in the world. Called the "Weebly Wanderlust" program, the intent is to support and encourage employees to travel, expand their world-views and check off goals from their bucket lists. By paying for both the time off and the flight, the company has gone that one step further to help them do just that.

According to David Rusenko, CEO and co-founder, "We want to show our employees that we value them and their work. It sends out the message that employees shouldn't feel they have to switch jobs to get the time off they need to recharge. At Weebly, we're all about helping our customers realize their dreams of starting their own businesses. With the Wanderlust program, we're giving our employees a chance to explore their own passions and dreams, knowing that when they come back, they will be so much more productive and refreshed."

What are employees doing with the benefit? One employee took her husband and two young children on a once-in-a-lifetime Wanderlust trip to major cities in Europe:

> "I think the best part about the opportunity is that I had the time to unplug, be present and spend time with my kids while they still wanted to hang out with me. I also got to blow their minds by showing them countries and cultures so far out of their wildest imagination and their comfort zones. All this while I know I have my role at Weebly to come back to. It shows we value our employees' commitment and know that it's healthy to step away and come back refreshed and renewed."

This benefit has made—and will make—a difference in the lives of Weeblies, preventing burnout by giving them enough time to truly relax and recharge. At the same time, it gives Weebly employees who are more engaged and productive, and who want to stay with the company. A great example of a win–win situation.

In Practice

- When looking for ideas for new benefits, find ones such as this that create not just engagement, but *long-term* engagement. Thanks to lasting memories from their trips, employees will think fondly of the company time and time again.

- Don't shy away from benefits such as sabbaticals, paid or unpaid. They often cost your company nothing and can provide much-needed rest and relaxation.

13

Building it

In Summary

We absolutely loved writing this book, developing the ideas we'd formed and meeting hundreds of tremendously brave and talented HR and leadership rebels around the world. It's been truly inspiring seeing the passion and dedication behind so much effort and ingenuity to make work better. We've learned such a lot on the journey and as we completed this stage, three things really stood out.

Maybe We've Forgotten What We Learned as Children

The first was how much the elements of the Engagement Bridge™, the components that make for an engaging culture, are actually things we learned in childhood. But then somehow we forgot them when we came to work or maybe left them at home. Things like telling the truth, trusting people, admitting it when you are wrong and being kind to people. We were left wondering how we'd gotten to a place where we forgot those things at work, or somehow thought they didn't apply.

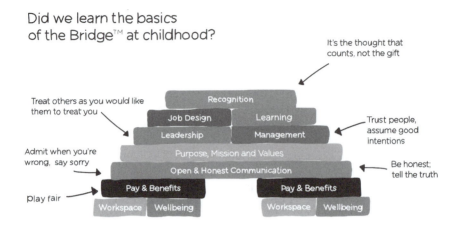

Did we learn the basics
of the Bridge™ at childhood?

At least this makes you realize that the things we need to do to make our workplaces more engaging aren't that difficult.

> *"Instinct, intuition and the golden rule of treating people as you want to be treated."*
>
> —Producer and Director
> JJ Abrams on how he manages people

So Much of the Bridge™ is Intertwined

It's hard to pull Leadership away from Open & Honest Communication—how can you deliver great leadership without that? The biggest problems with Pay are actually around fairness and that links us back to good leadership and communication too. Recognizing people properly needs them to be visible, leaning on a culture of good communication and they both improve social cohesion, building the relationships in your company.

Everywhere we looked, we saw connection and links, making it hard to actually decide which chapters some of the plays should go in. That highlights something very important in the Engagement Bridge™ model—**that it is a guide, not a manual; a lens through which to look, not a recipe**. Use the model to guide you, to look at your organization and its relationship with people from several angles. But don't worry about or get hung up on which intervention, change or fix lies specifically in which area—all that matters is that you are making your organization better, treating your people in a more human, more constructive way.

Together, in direct or subtle ways, each element touches and works with the others. Keep this in mind as you embark on your engagement journey, because understanding this connectivity is critical to you achieving what you set out to do.

Rebels Fundamentally Treat Their People Differently

Finally, the more companies we researched, the more certain we were that, to be successful, you do need to fundamentally change how your business operates in regard to your people.

To put it bluntly, in many businesses, a lot of our HR and management policies and procedures are disengaging. They were built around the belief that people are bad and the company has to be protected from them. You can buy the best tools and software, but you have to first start with the fundamental understanding that traditional business practice disengages people and it, and you, need to change them.

The rebels we met understand this. They trust their people as individuals, give them a voice and freedom, and allow then to do great work. If someone breaches that trust, they deal with that person as an individual rather than restricting freedom for the whole workforce.

Getting Started

Wherever you're starting from, whether you're an established company or a startup, the most important thing is to get moving and start making changes. Ultimately, when you start consciously working on employee engagement, you're going to have to make many small choices across the 10 areas of the Bridge™. The sum—the output—of those choices is going to be your culture.

This means you have to figure out in advance, as much as possible, what kind of culture your organization needs: What your unique situation warrants and, therefore, what your guiding North Star is. For Netflix, it is "A great place to work is awesome colleagues." For Amazon, it is an "intense focus on the customer through brave leadership." What will it be for you? The choice is critical because many paths are possible, but you need to follow through and reflect on your choice throughout the Bridge™ to make it work.

Overall, culture comes from the top. To make a real difference throughout a whole organization, it has to be owned by the CEO and the leadership team. It is then delivered, reinforced, damaged or destroyed on a daily, weekly and monthly basis by the policies you adopt, the managers in your organization and the choices that they make.

HR can and should have a strong role. They can be the champion of culture as a tool for business improvement; they can provide training, technology and resources that managers can use; and, most importantly, they can provide measurement and feedback. Knowing what your people are talking about, how they feel and what decisions they respect and which they think suck is key to building and retaining a strong culture that works for your organization.

Make Some Rebel Friends

We learned, in writing this book, that you can't be a rebel on your own. We moved mountains by discussing ideas together and we were hugely inspired and led by the hundreds of rebels we met and interviewed around the world. We hope you will go to the book's website, **rebelplaybook.com**, and connect with more rebels. Start finding your friends and rebel-advocates internally and get them to read this book, too. That's how to start building your rebel army.

We hope this book and the plays illustrating its various concepts will give you inspiration and ideas you can put in place quickly. To help you get started, there is a downloadable starter pack on the website, full of videos and tools to help explain things to others and a workshop pack you can work through.

Your next steps could be:

1. **Assess your organization**

   Look at each of the 10 elements of the Bridge™ and assess what changes should be made at your organization to improve employee engagement. Ask yourself the hard questions. Look at the plays in each chapter and ask, "Why couldn't I do this?" "What is stopping us?" "How could this look at my organization?"

2. **Assemble your rebel army**

   Think about the people close to you or senior to you whom you need on-side to make an impact, and make them a part of your "rebelution."

   > *"I can do things you cannot. You can do things I cannot. Together we can do great things."*
   >
   > —Mother Teresa

3. **Together, write your own playbook**

   Remember: No two organizations are the same, so build a strategy that works for you and is uniquely you.

   > *"There are risks and costs to action. But they are far less than the long-range risks of comfortable inaction."*
   >
   > —John F. Kennedy

We hope this book leaves you a little uncomfortable and a little restless for change; that was our goal. Remember, the Bridge™ model has an inherent bias for action, so now it's up to you to get going!

And tell us how you get on. We'd love to see your pictures, videos, comments and ideas—whatever rebellious actions you take yourselves—on Facebook, LinkedIn, Instagram or Twitter (**@rebelplaybook**) or via e-mail (rebels@rebelplaybook.com). Send them to us and we'll feature some of them on the website.

Glenn & Debra

@glennelliott and @debracoreyrebel

You can download a free **Build Your Playbook** to help you get started with the Bridge™, including videos, team exercises and templates from **rg.co/buildit-workshop**.

Join the "Rebelution"!
We need your feedback!
How can we make this book better?
Which Rebel should we meet next?

Which Rebel Playbook do you want to see next?
Employee Communications
Recognition
Pay & Benefits
Management
Entrepreneurship
rg.co/rebelfeedback

Find dozens more plays, interviews, chapter summaries and other content at
www.rebelplaybook.com.

Get the Rebel Playbook podcast on iTunes, Soundcloud, Podcaster or at rg.co/podcast.

Want Glenn or Debra to speak at your event, meet the board or run a workshop?
We can help.
rg.co/rebelution

Acknowledgments

Thanks first, obviously, to all the amazing HR, leadership rebels, CEOs and entrepreneurs whom we interviewed and featured in this book and the website—you were and are an inspiration, and we're so grateful you took the time to share your stories.

We are hugely grateful to all of the 359 staff at Reward Gateway who helped and contributed in many ways, but especially to our subject matter experts Rowenna Berry and Kylie Terrell on Recognition; Lucy Tallick on Wellbeing; Zach Wilkinson and Didi Kirova on Learning; and Kylie Green and James Edwards on all things Pay & Benefits, Recognition and Australia. Shelley Packer was an inspiration on Leadership, while Catrin Lewis and Charlie Taylor kept us honest with Communications and focused on Purpose, Mission & Values. Cover design, branding and all illustrations are all thanks to the hugely talented Sevi Rahimova and Leonie Williamson. For the book's website, we owe thanks to Rade Georgiev. Rob Hicks and Jonathan Burg supported us throughout. Thanks to Owen Davies and Samantha Marrazzo, who "owned it" on our Glassdoor analysis. Thanks to all of our external reviewers who saw the book in an awful, messy state, especially to Jane Vivier.

Special thanks to our editor at Reward Gateway, Chloe DeIulis, who worked with us for many months, and to Ruth E. Thaler-Carter, our copyeditor in New York, who worked to awful deadlines—both did their very best to correct as much of our terrible punctuation and grammar as was humanly possible. Errors that remain were almost certainly added by Glenn after Ruth's final review (Debra was away teaching by then, so we can't blame her).

Very special thanks to our lead internal reviewers Rob Boland and Doug Butler, whose time, skill and candid feedback improved so many chapters and challenged us to be more rebellious.

This book was only possible because of the wonderful journey we had at Reward Gateway, learning so much about employee engagement and meeting so many amazing people over 11 years, so we're grateful to the co-founders at Reward Gateway: Chris Whitcombe, Helen Craik, Charlie Murphy and Rizwan Kanval. You should all be proud that you started something that has permanence and meaning, and that you gave it the nurturing, loving start it needed in life.

from Glenn:

I'd like to thank Helen Craik, who was Reward Gateway's founding HR Director. With a lifetime of experience in HR and many hilarious stories involving milkmen at Express Dairies and running check-in at British Airways, Helen taught me all the basics of HR and people management during our four years together. This included some of the most-important founding principles of how to treat people at work that we have used and developed ever since. While the Engagement Bridge™ may have come much later, the seeds of honesty and transparency, communication and context, treating people well while still valuing high performance, and sharing success and wealth with employees were all Helen's. I'm also grateful to Tracy Mellor, who helped me to develop those ideas in the years that followed.

I'm hugely grateful to Andy Vaughan, Reward Gateway's Chairman from 2010 to 2015, for his patience and understanding as I developed from an upstart of an entrepreneur to a slightly more mature CEO and leader (I was an unpredictable and rebellious student). I'm also grateful to my friend and first investor Christian Hamilton at Tenzing for believing in me and the business when we were both young, fragile and rather stupid, and for my second investor, Chris Busby at Great Hill, for his patience, support and faith in me during my time as CEO and especially that rocky first 18 months.

And finally to my mum for always being there and my dad, Joe, who taught me to always be nice to people. But especially to my wonderful husband Kristian for his love, patience, understanding, and putting up with the craziness. Thanks for waiting for me babes.

from Debra:

I'd like to first thank Glenn, who surprised and delighted me when he asked that I partner in writing this book. It has been an absolute pleasure working with him on what I believe is a book that can and will change how we treat our people, making a profound difference in the world. I've learned so much throughout this journey, being pushed and challenged to think in ways I never thought my mind would stretch, and I will forever hear the voice of Glenn in my ear saying, "Why can't you do that?" I am confident that this will make me a better HR leader and a better person, and for that I am profoundly grateful.

Next, I'd like to thank the people who helped shape me throughout my very rewarding career as an HR professional. They include Eva-Sage Gavin, Bill Tompkins, Matt Martin, Dan Baker, Steve Foster, Tea Colaianni and Kate Chapman. You helped me move from seeing things in black and white to seeing things in color, and for that I will be forever grateful.

And last but not least, a huge thanks to my lovely husband Ken, who not once made me feel guilty as I worked nights and weekends on the book, instead jumping in and taking care of everything and everyone. My daughter Chloe and son Anthony, too, were supportive, even patiently listening as I went on and on about the great interview I had just had. Thank you all for your help and encouragement, you all rock!

With much love,
Glenn & Debra

Index